My Stories, All True

Publication of this book is generously supported by
Amy and Tim Leach in appreciation of J. David Bamberger
and his vision, energy, and commitment to the cause of land
restoration. He is truly leaving the world a better place.

My Stories, All True

J. David Bamberger
on Life as an
Entrepreneur and Conservationist

PAMELA A. LEBLANC

TEXAS A&M UNIVERSITY PRESS ◦ COLLEGE STATION

This paper meets the requirements of
ANSI/NISO Z39.48–1992 (Permanence of Paper).
Binding materials have been chosen for durability.
Printed in Canada by Friesens

LIBRARY OF CONGRESS CATALOGING-IN-PUBLICATION DATA
Names: Bamberger, J. David, 1928– author. | LeBlanc,
Pamela A., 1964– author.
Title: My stories, all true : J. David Bamberger on life as an entrepreneur
and conservationist / Pamela A. LeBlanc.
Other titles: J. David Bamberger on life as an entrepreneur and
conservationist
Description: First edition. | College Station : Texas A&M University Press,
[2020] | Includes index.
Identifiers: LCCN 2019052190| ISBN 9781623498849 (cloth) |
ISBN 9781623498856 (ebook)
Subjects: LCSH: Bamberger, J. David, 1928—Interviews. | Wildlife
rehabilitation—Texas—Bamberger Ranch Preserve. |
Conservationists—Texas—Blanco County—Biography. |
Bamberger Ranch
Preserve (Tex.)—History.
Classification: LCC F392.B18 B38 2020 | DDC 976.4/64063092 [B] —dc23

Dedication

In memory of my father, Edward Coleman.
I wish you could have met David.

None of this you read here
may ever have happened,
but it's all true.

—J. DAVID BAMBERGER

David and Pam pose after a fall color tour at Selah, November 2013.
Photo by Tino Mauricio.

CONTENTS

ACKNOWLEDGMENTS

I am forever grateful to J. David Bamberger and Joanna Rees for sharing their stories and parts of their lives with me. Many thanks to the Selah team, especially Colleen Gardner, Steven Fulton, Lois Sturm, and Jared Holmes, for making me feel welcome at the ranch; West Hansen for endless cups of tea; Ed Crowell, Pete Szilagyi, and Sharon Chapman, for reminding me I could do this; Marcy Stellfox for the sessions; Tino Mauricio and Rudy Gonzalez for the photos; and Shannon Davies and Patricia Clabaugh at Texas A&M University Press for making this happen. A special thank you goes to my family, Mary Lou Coleman, Diane Coleman, Angela Pierce, and Nancy Purifoy, for the quiet support they gave me; and to Chris LeBlanc for loving me so well.

My Stories, All True

David shows off a book he has just finished reading, early 2019. Photo by Pam LeBlanc.

Meet J. David Bamberger

When I first met J. David Bamberger in 2007, he charged to the top of a hilltop on his Blanco County ranch and threw his arms in the air like a tent-revival preacher. "Hallelujah!" he shouted, addressing a small troop of guests, mainly Texas Parks and Wildlife Department employees who were trying hard to keep up with him as he trotted upward, inspecting a series of low-stacked rock berms snaking around that ridgeline. The berms, he explained to his audience, some of whom were huffing and puffing a bit from the climb, slowed runoff and allowed the land to soak up more water, all part of his master plan to capture as much of the rain that fell on the ranch as possible. Then he pointed a few hundred yards down the hill, where water percolated out of a pipe at the rate of about a gallon per minute. "You see the evidence coming right out of the earth!" he proclaimed.

David, a former door-to-door vacuum cleaner salesman who had become a millionaire when he and his business partner built the Church's Chicken empire starting in the 1960s, bought the rural oasis he calls Selah, Bamberger Ranch Preserve in 1969. He intentionally picked out the most overgrazed, damaged ranchland he could find, paying $124 an acre for the first three thousand–acre purchase of the eroded, rocky parcel, overgrown with Ashe juniper, known commonly as cedar, and cactus and other woody species.

When he bought it, experts from conservation organizations, including the Sierra Club and several chapters of the Audubon Society, counted just 48 species of birds on its worn-out pastures, ridges, and fields. Today, he says, 218 different types of birds live on the now-lush property. He credits that increase in diversity to the restoration of the land. The native grasses he planted drew insects, which brought in birds to scratch through the grass to eat them. Those grasses also slowed the evaporation and runoff of water, and in time, long-dry springs began flowing, luring in more wildlife. Walk the ranch before the sun rises and you will likely encounter turkeys trotting across golden fields, owls hooting from their perches on old oak trees whose branches stretch to the sky, deer hopping over creek beds, and, if you are lucky (or not), a skunk waddling into the woods.

"Grass is the best conservation tool there is," David said while we sat in his guesthouse at Selah one fall afternoon talking about the changes that had come to the place in the preceding half century, "the cheapest, easiest, and quickest to produce. It saves water and soil and supports all wildlife."

David wanted to share that knowledge and insisted that landowners did not have to be millionaires to nudge overgrazed or abused property back to health. He ranks as near legendary in conservation circles today for how he replanted native grasses and trees and managed livestock more carefully, ultimately reviving his little corner of the Texas Hill Country near Johnson City. But what most captured me about David, who was eighty when I first met him, was the magic he worked on people. He drew you in; he made you care. Spend a morning at Selah, Bamberger Ranch Preserve and you will find yourself plotting to stop on a highway median in the Hill Country some afternoon to collect grass seeds, which you will then plant on your land to hold in water and promote native vegetation.

"I believe in speaking the word, the gospel of conservation," he said. A big part of David's gospel involved saving water, and visitors were always treated to a demonstration of how native grasses encourage water retention and hold soil in place with their tangled roots.

Since that first meeting, I have spent hours driving around the ranch with David and plenty more sitting in his workroom amid stacks of books, papers, and clippings, listening to him tell me the story of his life.

If we were driving the ranch in his old pickup truck (David scoffed at anyone who bought a new car; he reminded you how much more sense it made to buy a used one), he would screech to a halt in front of a pond, leap out, and tell me how he once convinced a trailer full of visitors that he had trained the catfish living there to rise to the surface at his command. He pointed out a bank full of cypress trees and explained that he had planted hundreds of them in a single hour. He coasted down narrow farm roads, trying to roll as far as possible without hitting the gas. He would say crazy things, like "Would you like to see the bridge on the River Kwai?" and park the truck, lead you down a narrow pathway to a footbridge that looks nothing like the bridge made famous in that 1957 movie about World War II, and then explain how he and his staff dragged the structure down through the brush and trees and installed it there themselves.

David climbs into his well-loved Toyota pickup truck, late summer 2017. Photo by Rodolfo Gonzalez.

Then he kept on walking, pointing out trees he has planted and plants he has cultivated, until he got to a beautiful alcove, where a cluster of tree trunks grew out of a single gnarled base. In front of that tree, he knelt down and pulled back grasses that lap like waves over a plaque on a stone-lined gravesite. His wife, Margaret, was buried there in the shade of that oak. He credited much of what happened at the ranch to Margaret, whom he described as the best naturalist he had ever known. On the way back to the car, he pointed out a natural cedar break, a section of cedars that stand shoulder to shoulder without much brush beneath their dark green needles.

Bamberger has removed many of the water-sucking cedars from his property but leaves them where they would have occurred historically. This is golden-cheeked warbler country, and the endangered birds use bark from the mature trees to build their nests. "I left this on purpose starting forty-eight years ago, maybe because it was so thick. I'm so glad I did. This is a wonderful place for wildlife," he says.

The grove provided a place for animals to seek shelter in

David walks through a grove of cedar trees at Selah, late summer 2017. Photo by Rodolfo Gonzalez.

storms. Its shady recesses also served as protection from predators for wildlife moving from one part of the ranch to another. He pointed out the oddly bent branches of some of the trees in the copse, explaining that a windstorm swept through at one point, tearing at the trees' arms and twisting their branches. He showed me Lacey oaks and Eve's necklace, his blue eyes brightening at the wonder of each one.

And that was the thing about David. This man, who saw so much success in the business world and could tell stories about dining with Lady Bird Johnson, rubbing shoulders with Jane Goodall, making deals with Walmart mogul Sam Walton, and speaking to business executives around the world, bubbled with excitement at the sight of a pretty flower or a lush field of grass. He grinned when he talked about the snakes, lizards, and hummingbirds that live on his fifty-five hundred-acre ranch. That passion infected the people he met.

He turned ninety years old on June 11, 2018, and told me more than once that he was worried this book would not be finished before he dies. So I spent as many weekends out there as I could to listen to his stories and write down what he wants people to know about his life. After he dies, he said, a retired pilot named David Grey has agreed to take his ashes up in an airplane and spread them around the ranch. He will fly low and scatter that dust over the land that taught David so much about what it takes to return damaged land to health. That sounded perfect. It is where Bamberger's soul will keep on living—and his stories will keep inspiring.

"I have no complaints," he said. "It's been such a wonderful life."

Those stories? They are all at least rooted in fact, although David is quick to admit some may be stretched just a tad or missing a few facts as he remembered them. "None of this may ever have happened, but it's all true," he said. "I'm a storyteller. I may have enhanced them to make them more interesting."

1

Childhood

In 2017, I headed to Selah as often as I could, armed with a tape recorder and a laptop computer. David and I would retreat to his workroom at the ranch house, where he flipped through books and notes and letters, telling me stories about his life. We would pause and gaze out the window. You could not see any buildings or roads or signs of development up there, just hummingbirds and wildflowers and hills that unfolded like rumpled green and tan blankets all the way to the horizon. To be honest, it was a respite for me. As much as David protested about filling my weekends with more work, I needed to come out to Selah, just like he needed its calming vistas and healing breezes. I was a staff reporter at the *Austin American-Statesman* at the time, where I wrote about fitness and adventure travel. My world has always been fast paced and deadline driven, and I travel all the time. That is not a bad thing in itself. I cannot sit still, ever, and the job kept me exploring and discovering new things. Still, it was stressful.

But there was more. My father had died of nonsmoker's lung cancer late in 2014. My mother, who lived in Michigan, was struggling with confusion, depression, and a slow-moving form of

Pam interviews David in his workroom, summer 2017. Photo by Chris LeBlanc.

leukemia. She refused to move to assisted living and my two sisters and I lived hundreds of miles away. The best we could do was take turns visiting her and attempt to deal with the endless series of crises from afar.

I felt different, too. In August 2016, my husband, Chris, and I had spent fifteen days backpacking the John Muir Trail in California. As challenging as that was—and I remember one particular moment when I stopped on a trail halfway up a mountain pass and nearly gave up because getting to the top of it, and the next half dozen passes after it, felt so impossible—it taught me something. From the side of the mountain, the lake we had started hiking from that morning glinted like a dime far below. Chris pointed to it to encourage me. As cliché as it sounds, I realized that just by scrambling over one sharp-edged, shin-busting rock at a time, I could climb that mountain pass and the next one. I could finish the hike no matter what the trail threw at me, be it bashed toes, terrifyingly sheer cliffs, or never-ending climbs with supplies strapped to my back.

That experience flipped a switch in my brain. When I got back to Texas, I suddenly wanted to embrace everything that made my pulse race, without being reckless. I needed to leap into ice-cold lakes and jump off high dives. I needed to swim in the ocean with sharks, camp solo, and canoe the Devils River in West Texas. And also, I needed to write.

The newspaper accommodated and publicly proclaimed my "Year of Adventure." I set to work, ticking off one dare after the next. I ran a naked 5K race wearing nothing but shoes and a straw cowboy hat. I rappelled down a thirty-eight-story downtown Austin building dressed in a Wonder Woman costume. I scuba dived and trail ran, climbed rocky cliffs on nearby Lake Travis, ran a nighttime adventure race, and spoke in public about all of it.

Writing a book about David would be just one more assignment to tackle, but it scared me more than any other. How could I ever record all those stories, or fact-check the details, or explain the science behind what David was doing out at Selah? The John Muir Trail held the answer. The only way to write a book was to take that first step up the mountain. And on this day, crouched over a laptop in David's workroom, I wanted to know more about where he came from.

J. David Bamberger did not grow up rich. He grew up in modest surroundings in northern Ohio, and the idea that he would one day become a wealthy man seemed about as likely as plucking a fist-sized diamond from one of the trees that grew in the woods around his childhood home. In short, it was absurd—except that David practically willed it to happen.

David's mother, Hester, was orphaned as a girl. She left Hartford City, Indiana, as a teenager and enrolled in a nursing program in Massillon, Ohio. There, she met Titus Bamberger. The couple married and three boys were born—Louis James, Thomas Anthony, and John David. For a while, Titus made a lean living selling Essex and Hudson automobiles, but when World War II broke out, the supply of cars dried up. With nothing to peddle, he took a job as a guard in a steel mill in Massillon, fifty miles south of Cleveland.

While David was still a young boy, the family moved into a small shack without running water or electricity, seven miles outside the town. The home stood a few miles from the intersection of two railroad lines, an important landmark for David. An attendant there operated a tiny blockhouse the size of an outdoor toilet, as David describes it, that stood alongside the track. When a train rumbled down one track, the attendant waved a flag to alert any other trains on the other track of the coming traffic. In David's eyes, anyone who worked for the railroad had landed a fine job. From an early age, he recognized that other families had things that his did not.

David read what he could get his hands on, and one book he remembered, *T-Model Tommy*, told the story of a young man who bought a Ford truck and used it to build a successful trucking business. "I remember he was just a boy," David says of the book's main character, from whom he drew inspiration. "He was poor, but he worked and saved his money. I tell you what. I saved money, too."

On occasions when David mingled with other kids, he paid close attention to the comforts they enjoyed. When he was five or six, a friend invited him to stay a few nights in town. What made the biggest impression during that visit was not the friend but the food David was served by his friend's mother. At the

David holds family photos of him and his brothers as boys in Ohio. Photo by Pam LeBlanc.

breakfast table in the morning, he found himself face-to-face with a banana and a real live bowl of prepackaged Rice Krispies with milk instead of the homemade, extra-crunchy, granola-type cereal his own mother made from scratch. "God," David said. "Those were things I thought all the rich people ate." David talked often about the food his mother served, and while he may not have appreciated that cereal at the time, he now looks back with fondness on the nuts, fruits, and greens she foraged to feed the family.

He also quickly learned the value of water. "People ask me all the time, 'When did you become a conservationist?'" he says now. He responds with a funny story. When he was a small boy, the family did not have a water well. David's job was to walk a quarter of a mile to a neighbor's house, carrying the same bucket that was used to milk the cow. "When you're a four- or five-year-old kid and sent down a dirt road to a neighbor, and you have to pump a bucket full of water and carry it up a hill, and by the time you get it home your pants are wet and your bucket is half empty—that's when you learn to become a conservationist," he says.

At Selah, David knew the value of water. He tracked rainfall and could tell you the last time any significant amount fell on Madrone Lake, the glimmering spring-fed pool on the ranch that serves as a sort of watery exclamation point to all he has done here. He worked hard not to waste a drop. Often, he drew on lessons he learned as a boy growing up in Ohio.

When David was old enough to go to school, he and his brothers walked to a one-room brick schoolhouse, which had a sliding door to separate the lower four grades from the higher grades and a single teacher to teach the entire student population. When David entered first grade, he was the only student in his grade; later on, a set of triplets joined him.

David attended school in that one-room schoolhouse until sixth grade, when the district consolidated and opened a modern, new, two-story building to serve the region. Not always the best-behaved student, he received a whipping one day after he called one of the campus teachers, whose last name was Broomie, "broomstick." In return, David says, that teacher trimmed a branch off a tree and "whipped the shit out of me." He did not dare tell his parents, because he knew he would be punished again if they heard what he had done.

When the Rural Electrification Act passed in 1936, power lines began crisscrossing the countryside, slowly reaching farms and homes like the Bambergers' outside urban centers. Other improvements were taking place, too. Crews paved the dirt road that led to the Bamberger home.

"Those days, those times in the country, as poor as we were and as poor as everybody was, were some of the best days of my life," Bamberger said.

But when David was twelve, his father died in an industrial accident, crushed when a crane collapsed at a steel mill where he was a security guard. Not long after that, David's oldest brother, Jim, five years his senior, was shot down while flying over the English Channel in a B-26. Jim's body—and that of the plane's pilot—was never found, although the bodies of two crewmembers washed up on shore. David's mother lost her husband and eldest son in close succession, and her second son, Thomas, left to join a navy program at an Ohio university. At home, it was just Hester and David.

"Two things I want to say right here," David says. "For years I've regretted and am somewhat ashamed that I was such a smart-aleck kid, but I had no understanding whatsoever of the pain my mother went through, losing her husband and oldest son within a year and a half."

One thing, though, he did know for sure: He wanted better circumstances in his life as an adult than he had as a kid. Those childhood experiences aimed him like a rocket to the future. At thirteen, when David started shaving, he would wet a bristle brush, swirl it around on a cake of soap, and slather it over his face. A mirror hung on the wall in front of the bathroom sink, and when he finished shaving, he took that soapy brush and wrote a dollar sign on the mirror. Something in the soap etched a permanent mark on the mirror's glass, a dollar sign that never faded.

After a while, his mother noticed. "Davy, quit that," she said. "Why are you writing on that mirror?" He told her the angry truth, as he saw it. He told her he kept writing that dollar sign to remind himself he did not want to be poor when he grew up. He did not want to live the way he was living then.

Early on, David thought he wanted to become an electrician, a carpenter, or a plumber. He also did not understand the way hiring took place. "I thought I could walk in and say, 'I'd like a job,'" he says. Sometimes, his ignorance worked in his favor. He tracked down the man in charge of a cemetery one summer and told him he would like to work there mowing the lawn. The cemetery manager agreed, handing over the reins of a push mower and a pair of big clippers. David used the money he earned to buy himself a Model A Ford coupe with a rumble seat.

While circumstances instilled in David a drive to pull himself out of poverty, David's mother also influenced him at an early age with her respect for and appreciation of nature. She particularly loved anything by the writer Louis Bromfield, a Pulitzer Prize–winning novelist and author of the book *Pleasant Valley*. She gave a copy of the book to David and encouraged him to read it. "It motivated me," David says. "Every once in a while, we get touched by something. That book touched me."

Bromfield's story would serve as a blueprint for what David ended up doing decades later. The writer had spent time working on his grandparents' farm in Ohio when he was a boy. Later, he moved to France, where he learned about land conservation and the importance of things like crop rotation in keeping soil productive. When World War II broke out, Bromfield left Europe and returned to the United States. He drove into the hills of Ohio, looking for his grandparents' place. He eventually found the farm, but years of misuse had rendered it worn out, brush covered, and nearly useless. Bromfield bought the farm anyway, along with three adjacent parcels of land, and turned his attention to habitat restoration. He demonstrated a knack for the work and chronicled it in his writing.

Bromfield's farm stood only thirty-five miles from where David grew up, and Hester drove her boys there to see it. (It later became Malabar Farm State Park, which David visited years later, noting its commercialization with much disdain: "To me, it's sad, because everybody puts in a lot of cheap Chinese-made plastic junk. They turned the garage into a gift shop.")

David read Bromfield's book many times and tucked his well-worn copy into his belongings when he entered the US Army after graduating from high school. That book—and his simple upbringing—turned out to have a lasting impact.

Betting on a Horse

David described his father, Titus, as a hardworking man who often worked late, first as a railroad clerk, then as a car salesman, and later as a guard at the steel mill. But Titus also frequented local bars and gambled, which sometimes led to tension at home.

That gambling streak played a role in one story David shared about a pony named Dolly. Dolly gave him the freedom to stretch his leash farther from home, to go off on his own to seek adventure. But David harbored a little guilt about having that pony, too. Neither of his brothers had a horse. And looking back, he recognized that his mother could have used the money spent to care for the animal on things the family needed. It became a sticking point with David's parents.

I was born in Ann Arbor, Michigan, but moved to Austin when I was four or five. Back then, I imagined Texas as a place where everyone rode a horse to school and tumbleweeds bounced down gravel roads. When I got here, I figured out that was not necessarily the case, but I got my horseback fix anyway. My parents paid for me and my two older sisters to take riding lessons once every two weeks. My mom would drive us to a small ranch just outside the city limits, where we saddled up and practiced training drills in an oval arena. On really special days, we took the horses out and ran them up and down a pasture or even left the property and trotted them a few miles down the road to Decker Lake.

For me, that was living the dream—or as close to it as I had ever come. Because sharing an adventure with a living, breathing animal that could carry you down the road or into a creek or up a hillside, one that would munch an apple or a carrot and warm you up if you buried your hands in its thick hair on a chilly day, was better than driving a car any day.

David rode some when he first bought Selah, and he had a few tales to spin about that. Except for the horses his ranch hands use to work cattle, he does not keep horses other than a retired old horse named Max who spent his last few years on the property and had to be put down the Christmas I was working on the book.

﹏⋱⁄⋰﹏

We lived way out in Nowhereville, and we lived pretty simply. Two or three cars a day came down that dirt road and not much else. But when I was seven or eight years old, my dad got me a pony. Dolly was white with a black spot. My dad had a horse, too, and both animals lived in an old log barn across the dirt road. I went over and fed them and took care of them every day. My brothers didn't have ponies, and I think that created some problems. My mom didn't have things that other boys' mothers had, and my dad had a horse and I had a pony when what we really needed was a washing machine. I remember hearing them fight because he had to buy oats for the horses and she didn't have enough money for the family.

I loved Dolly like a man loves a dog. She gave me the freedom that a man of sixteen gets today from a car. You could get on a pony and go anywhere. I never packed a lunch, either, because I could just hop off and pick a berry from a roadside bush or find nuts from a tree. I remember sneaking into our neighbor's orchards and getting apples and cherries. I could catch her easily by calling her up almost like a dog. I got to be a pretty darn good rider, too. I never used a saddle; I'd just throw a rope over Dolly's nose. I used to play like I was an Indian, and once I even tried to build a canoe by cutting the bark off a birch tree.

When my dad was home on Sundays, we'd head out riding. We'd go out on these old country roads, and sometimes we'd go to a place called Brook Field Country Club, a golf course. It took an hour and a half to ride over there, but I always got an orange soda pop. I'd ride all day for that. We did that one time, and on the way back we stopped by somebody's farm so my dad could take a look at some horses. In Ohio, farmers turn their cows out in the barnyard in the wintertime. That's what this was. A bunch of men were standing around talking about this farmer's horses and what makes a good one. The farmer brought one out to show us, and one of the men climbed onto it. The horse threw him off right away.

The men got to talking, and they decided if that old boy couldn't ride that particular horse, nobody could. That's when my dad raised his hand. "This boy can," he said, pointing to me. "Can you ride him, David?" I told him I could. The men placed bets, and my dad put me up on that horse.

The horse immediately started bucking like hell. I couldn't have been more than seven or eight years old, and that horse tossed me up in the air and the men started running for the fence. That horse kept bucking and didn't want to stop, but I grabbed its mane, and somehow I stuck on him. Finally, he stopped kicking. I still remember my dad going around to those men, collecting their money. He made about ten dollars, and he gave me one dollar of it.

"Davy, you did good," he told me afterward.

I don't think he ever told my mother. I know I didn't, because I didn't want to give up that dollar.

―ᐟ|ᐟ―

A Dime for a Movie

Some of my favorite stories from David were the ones he told about growing up in that humble shack in Ohio. I can easily picture him as a little kid, tumbling around with dirt streaking his pants and leaves tangled in his hair. He would shine bright as a copper penny one day, then turn into a scamp, doing something that ticked off his mother or father or schoolteacher the next.

He confessed lots of transgressions in short little tales that no

Jim, Tom, and David Bamberger as boys living in Ohio. Courtesy David Bamberger.

doubt evolved and changed a little every time he told them. Usually, he wove a little moral into each story. He would pull one or two of those gems out when school groups came to stay at Selah or adults came to learn about how they could follow David's lead and help restore their own land, even if it was a corner lot in a suburban neighborhood.

David's family didn't have much when he was a boy, so David and his brothers went outdoors for fun. They rambled up and down the nearby railroad tracks, they found inventive ways to make a few nickels, and they picked fruits and nuts from the land. When David told these stories, his voice changed. It got a little softer, and you could hear the admiration he felt for his mother. He opened his bright blue eyes wide and looked straight at me to make sure I got the point of each one.

David told his stories for a reason. Everything pointed toward his ultimate goal: to convince people to take responsibility for their actions, to reverse the damage people have done to the planet, to do the right thing, and to leave the land better than it was when we got here. As a stone gravestone that David had planted alongside the main road cutting through his ranch proclaims, "In memory of man. He who once dominated the earth destroyed it with his wastes, his poisons and his own numbers."

All this made me wish that I had been able to introduce my own father to David, because I think they would have had a lot to talk about. My dad grew up in Detroit, the son of a pressman on the daily newspaper. Even as a boy, my father was a mad scientist in training. He once brewed up a mysterious concoction in his basement science lab that splattered a mist of purple gel over the neighboring homes. Another time, he rigged a device so he could pump up a grape-sized bladder placed under his uncle's Thanksgiving dinner plate, slowly raising and tilting the plate until gravy spilled off the mashed potatoes. And my dad loved the land, too. He worked his urban Austin lot, planting native species and spreading so much mulch every spring that we joked about it. He did not want a groomed lawn with trimmed hedges. He left the back mostly wild, with cedar elms and redbuds dropping leaves onto slabs of limestone pocked like Swiss cheese.

I never got a chance to introduce them; my dad died two years before I dove into writing the book. I think he would have appreciated this story, because my dad taught me early on the importance of earning things rather than having them handed to you.

⁓⋅⎇⋅⁓

During the Depression, the five of us lived in a little rundown shack a mile from the school. Mom and Dad wanted to make the house more livable, so they were tearing down the interior walls, exposing the lathe—long slender sticks tacked to two-by-fours, which were then covered with plaster. As they disassembled that wall rib by rib, a pile of discarded bones grew in the yard—sticks of wood bristling with nails.

One day, a man came to our one-room schoolhouse

with a projector. He'd made arrangements with the teacher so the kids could see a movie. Nobody had radios, and televisions didn't exist, so it was a big thing, but it was going to cost ten cents to go see the film. That didn't matter. Everyone was going. My brothers earned one dollar a day working for the neighbor, so they planned to go see the movie. But I had to stay behind. I didn't have a cent.

My mom consoled me a little, then made a suggestion. "Davy, why don't you help me by getting a hammer and pulling those nails out of that lathe?" she said.

Everybody, it seemed, was going to see that movie. I wanted to go, too. But she persuaded me to stay and help her out. I took the hammer and went outside and started working. The way I remember it, I spent half a day out there, sorting through that pile, plucking out boards, yanking out nails, and dropping them into a coffee can. When I got to the bottom of the stack, I made a discovery: a dime, covered in dirt.

I couldn't believe it. I called for my mom, telling her what I'd found. Then I ran like hell to the school so I could see that movie, too. I don't even remember what they showed, but the lesson stayed with me all my life. The only place success comes before work is in the dictionary. If you work, though, good things can happen to you. It took years before I realized my mom had planted that dime, knowing I would find it, but also knowing I had to work hard to uncover it. It's a lesson that stayed with me my entire career.

—⁄|\—

Making a Buck

I never had to hike down to the railroad tracks to collect scrap metal to sell to a junkman or gather berries on the side of the road to earn a few extra pennies the way David did. I grew up in a middle-class family. Both my parents worked—my mother as a

David leans back and tells another story, late summer 2017. Photo by Rodolfo Gonzalez.

librarian, my father as an aeronautical engineer—and we always had whatever we needed. David, on the other hand, knew what it was like to scrape for money. He grew up during the Depression, and the lessons he learned applied throughout his life. Some people joked that David was cheap. That is fine with him. He scoffed at expensive hotels and luxury anything. He drove around in a well-worn, used Toyota pickup truck. He did live on a sprawling ranch, but his modest home was built decades ago. He was proud of how he could furnish a home with castoff items and things purchased from secondhand shops.

In February 2018, one of my good friends, Marcy, was single and living near Lampasas, working at a winery in Hye, a twenty-minute drive from Selah. Occasionally, to shorten her commute, she would drive out to the ranch and spend the night with me when I was there. She had popped over to the ranch to keep me company one night when David and his significant other, Joanna Rees, stopped by to say hi.

We opened a bottle of wine, as Marcy told David that she had just bought a house in Blanco. She was proud of her purchase and could not wait to move in. David took note. Then he had some advice to pass on. He waved his hand around the room, explaining that he had hardly paid a dime to decorate the guesthouse, this gorgeous limestone structure with a tall fireplace, wood-paneled walls, and windows that overlooked Bamberger's slice of the Texas Hill Country. The house sat on a ridge, pointed toward a ring of hills. You could not see a house or building or road without climbing up on the roof. A wide planked porch wrapped around two sides of the building, and in the summer we would sit out there, watching the light drain from the sky and the stars pop out like candlelight flickering behind a pinpricked velvet curtain.

"This table right here," he bragged, tapping the coffee table set between the two hand-me-down couches on which the four of us were perched, "eight dollars." We admired the table. "And those bar stools over there at the counter?" he said, as we trained our eyes on two tall wooden chairs that swiveled just like the ones you would find along the coffee bar at an old-school diner. "Six dollars each."

Piece by piece he moved around the room, telling us how little he had spent for each item: a pair of brown wicker chairs, practically free; the lamps, all donated; the pictures hanging from the wall, gifts. We cracked up a little each time he presented another item. But he made a good point. All perfectly cozy, perfectly functional items, and perfectly inexpensive. And by reusing stuff that had been cast off, we were saving resources needed to manufacture new things.

⁓⟋⟍

We were poor and didn't have much money. I had two older brothers, and a neighbor farmer would hire them for work just about any day they were available. I was too small, though, and couldn't do the work the farmer needed. Instead, Mom taught me ways to make some money of my own.

The first thing she did was show me the sassafras tree. Really, it was more of a bush. She told me to dig down to the roots and clip them off, then scrub the dirt off and peel them like you would a carrot. We'd tie those clean pieces into a bundle or wrap a rubber band around them. You could make sassafras tea with those roots. My dad took the bundles into town and sold them for fifty cents each.

Mom took me out in the woods in the springtime, too, and taught me how to collect mushrooms, taking care to show me which ones we could eat and which ones we couldn't. I'd hunt for two or three hours and sometimes find only a few mushrooms. But when I got a sack full, I'd take them back home and my dad would take them into town to sell, just like those sassafras roots.

We picked the wild blackberries that grew out in the woods and fields around our house, filling quart containers made of thin wood strips. We'd gather hazelnuts, too, and I ate more of them than you can imagine. All of it my dad took to town to sell.

I'd like to believe that I made more than my brothers' dollar a day. Sometimes, I'd tag along with my brothers. We were energetic and hardworking. We knew that the only way you got any money was to earn it.

An old Jewish junk buyer named Butch used to come by every six weeks to buy stuff from us. He didn't want tin, but he bought all the aluminum, zinc, and iron we could find, so we started rummaging around all the dumps out in the country. Nobody ever used the word "recycling" then. Every farmer just threw his junk in a gully. We'd rescue lids off Mason jars—those lids were made of zinc, and we'd break out the glass and save them by the bag full. We'd gather up old aluminum kitchen utensils, too, and dented pots people tossed out as worthless.

Butch would pay us four or five dollars for a big pile of scrap iron—a hell of a lot of money back then. We'd always find stuff for him, and we were proud of it. "I can always count on the Bamberger boys to have something for me," he told our mother.

One year my brothers discovered all kinds of iron lying around the railroad tracks. When trains came through on the Baltimore and Ohio line, they'd stop to wait for trains crossing on the Wheeling and Lake Erie line. They'd shed chunks of metal—broken brakes, pieces of machinery, and other odd parts. That stuff may as well have been gold to us.

We got a wheelbarrow with a steel wheel and wooden boards on the side and made the forty-five-minute walk down to the tracks. When we got there, we found pieces so big I couldn't lift them by myself. My brothers did all the hard work, stacking them in the wheelbarrow and pushing it once it was loaded, but I helped gather up all the stuff. Then we dropped our load on the side of the road and waited for Butch, wondering just how much money he'd give us for our treasure. Butch used a big scale to weigh everything out. We added it up in our heads beforehand, counting out in our minds how much we would earn.

"Now zinc is bringing fourteen cents a pound; iron's bringing this," Butch would say, putting it on his scale. Later that day, when Butch finally came around in his beat-up old truck and saw us, he knew what we had. He weighed the zinc and the aluminum, then picked out all those big, valuable pieces of iron. "Boys," he said, and I remember him putting his hand on my head. "I know you worked real hard, but I can't buy this. I can't buy it because it's against the law."

At first, we didn't understand. But he told us how some people had gotten so desperately poor that they'd go down to railroad cars with sledgehammers and knock stuff off parked trains so they could resell it. To stop it from happening, lawmakers had passed a law that prevented anybody from recycling iron that came off railroad cars.

We had to carry every bit of that iron back to the railroad tracks. We were disappointed but not entirely discouraged. As we rolled our load back down to the tracks, we discovered bushes filled with wild strawberries. We spotted another business opportunity and started picking those berries to make up for some of the money we'd lost from the iron. We brought the berries home and gave them to my dad. He took the strawberries—we'd picked four quarts of them—and sold them to customers who'd come in to look at cars at the lot where he worked. That didn't work out so well, either. Two days later, the people who'd bought the fruit came back to the dealership, all upset. Those berries were covered in so much coal dust—so much soot and grit—that nobody could eat them. My dad had to give them their money back.

Next we turned to critter control. The Department of Agriculture had instituted a program to control the populations of mice, rats, and sparrows. They paid ten cents for every mouse tail, a nickel for every sparrow head, and twenty-five cents for every dead rat. We'd creep around at night with a flashlight, hunting varmints. Neighbors who had cattle in their barn had big stacks of hay kicked out by their threshing machines. It looked like a giant explosion of hay. The cattle would eat from it, and sparrows would dive in there looking for loose grain. We'd reach in and grab a bird, twist its head off, and put it in our bag. We'd get loads of mice tails, rat tails, and sparrows. I kept an old trapping log to keep track of what I caught. One time I even entered in a muskrat, for four dollars. That was a ton of money.

Jackie's Ball Game

I knew as soon as I met him that David was the kind of guy you wanted to hang around with. He took serious stuff seriously, but he packed a good dollop of humor and fun into everything. Even just driving his old truck around the ranch, he would see how far he could coast without pressing his foot on the gas pedal. He would chew the fat with his poker buddies once a year or crack up at the antics of his tree-climbing dog, Cory. He would tell tale after tale about the tricks he played on people he worked with over the years.

He knew the value of play and understood that to get people to work hard, they had to have fun along the way. He also knew that if you do not play fair, others might take their ball and bat and leave. That was a lesson he learned early on, and one that he held close to his heart when it came to Selah. It was not just his land. He was setting it aside for the next generation. He wanted people to appreciate it, understand it, and take what they learned home with them to pass on to others.

⁓⁄⁓

During the Depression, most of us didn't have access to fancy manufactured toys, so we'd spend days playing kick the can, shooting marbles, and climbing trees. A boy named Jackie lived across the street. His dad worked for the railroad, a coveted position where you could earn decent money, and one day Jackie strolled out with a brand-new ball and bat his father had given him. We all got so excited—a kid on our street now had a real ball and bat, and now we could play a real game. Every boy in the neighborhood, all eight or nine of us, lined up on the curb to play.

Every day Jackie showed up, we picked teams, figured out game rules, and played. Talk about fun. We didn't have enough players for a real game, but the bat and ball made it feel real enough to us. Jackie, though, wasn't much of a ball player. He was my age and taller than me. But he couldn't hit or throw the ball, and he couldn't run fast enough around the bases. Whenever the boys got together to choose up sides, he got picked last. That didn't sit well.

One day, Jackie showed up with the ball and bat and announced that since he owned it, he'd be instituting some new rules. He'd get four strikes, while the rest of us got three. He'd have to run to the tree and back, but the rest of us had to run farther, all the way to the fence and back. Jackie got to name the teams, too.

"This is my ball and bat, and that's how it's going to work," he said. But it didn't work. Jackie's rules didn't improve his game-playing ability a bit—he still couldn't hit, pitch, catch, or run. And his rules took all the fun out of the game. Eventually one morning when Jackie walked up with his ball and bat, most of the guys had disappeared from the curb.

I learned something from that experience. If you own the ball and bat and don't share it, you'll play a lonely game. That's why I share my fifty-five hundred acres at Selah with thousands of people. More than twelve hundred landowners come to Selah every year to take educational courses, and thousands of children visit every year on school trips. My children won't inherit this ranch. It's here for everybody.

‾⁄₁∖‾

The Day David's Father Died

I learned what it feels like to lose your father not long after I turned fifty, something that David learned when he was a little boy. That makes me sad because even though my dad was nowhere near ready to go when he died in 2014 at the age of seventy-nine, I had collected a pretty full library of memories by then. David never had that luxury. I hope he felt the presence of his dad at times, the same way I still feel the presence of mine.

I used to describe my dad as book smart and intellectual, but in truth, he was also as goofy and awkward as a mad scientist. I can picture him perfectly, with a neatly trimmed beard and long sideburns, wearing brown socks with sandals and, back in the day, a fringed suede vest. My dad liked to tell stories about his boyhood the same way David told me stories about his childhood. My father, an aeronautical engineer who loved anything to do with outer space, became my own Captain Adventure for life, leading me on exploratory missions into the nature preserve at the end of our street, to parks around Texas, and later, all the way to England. We pitched tents at Inks Lake State Park, hiked the arroyos and mesas of Big Bend National Park, and ogled dinosaur tracks in the Texas Hill Country. He rode a raft down the Grand Canyon in the 1980s, something that inspired me to take a similar trip twenty-five years later.

He got crotchety and we snapped at each other sometimes, too, but "Big Ed," as we called him, filled my belly with a curiosity about the world around me. He instilled in me the importance of casting a ballot and verbalizing my opinion. He religiously read several newspapers and believed it was every person's responsibility to stay informed of what was happening in the world. If we did not, who would notice when things took a downhill dive? In other words, my dad was a lot like David. My dad no longer drops by my house on the way back from the plant nursery or calls me up to see how my day went. But he remains alive and well in my heart, and I see him in the stars at night. And when I started spending more time with David to write the book, a little piece of my dad reappeared in my life.

David stands for all the right things. He cares about the environment and how people treat it. He believes that people should be responsible for their actions. He acts silly sometimes and laughs and walks over fields and valleys, looking at everything with a little jolt of wonder, as if it is a special message sent to guide him on his way.

⁓⁓

During World War II, the car business dried up, so my dad got a job working at the steel mill. He patrolled the factory as a guard, walking around with a pistol on his hip. We had moved from the country back to the town of Massillon, Ohio, and I must have been in seventh or eighth grade at Longfellow Junior High School.

I remember so many details about that day, October 22, 1942. Our classroom had no air-conditioning, so all the windows were open. The school wasn't far from the local hospital, and as we were sitting in class, we started hearing sirens just coming and coming and coming. The kids twisted around in their seats to see what was going on and to find out if those were fire trucks or police cars roaring past. After a while, the sirens quieted down. We got back to work in the classroom. Chalk scraped across the blackboard. Papers shuffled.

Then, a little while later, two men came to the classroom door and called my teacher out into the hallway. She came back into the room and pulled me out of my seat. My dad. That day, as he had walked his route in the mill, an overloaded crane swung around and its shaft broke. A load of steel—maybe thirty or forty tons—fell on my dad from his hips on down.

They took me out of school and brought me to the hospital. Somebody showed me his shoe, which was smashed. He lived for twenty hours after the accident, and I got to talk to him before he died. He told me to listen to my mother. "You pay attention to her," he told me. But as a young boy, I had no idea what that meant or what I should do. I wasn't prepared for any of it. My dad was forty-two when he went, and he left behind my mother, who was also forty-two, and three boys. She got a small settlement of about forty-five thousand dollars—not enough to raise three children on her own. I was a problem, a hard kid to raise. If I had that to do over again, I'd be more attentive, more caring.

―⁄ι⌐

The Freedom of a Car

Remember when you got your first car? It meant freedom, on the level of a dog tethered to a stake in the backyard that finally slips its collar and bolts over the fence. Everyone has a story about his or her first car, including David, who prides himself on never buying a brand-new vehicle. ("It loses value the minute you drive it off the lot.") He found his first four-wheeled love tucked inside a weathered old barn in the country. He was too young to drive, but that did not matter.

When he told the following story, it reminded me of driving around Selah, riding shotgun next to him as he pointed the car down the narrow paved road and took his foot off the pedal. I held on tight at times like those and could not help thinking about another thing David told me—about times he blacked out, probably because he had not been drinking enough water that day. We rolled down the unfurling ribbon of the ranch road, and the countryside scrolled past, a blur of cactus, creeks, and tall, waving grass. I always hoped to God he was fully hydrated, and on all of those days, he was.

I remembered a little about my first driving experience, too. I loved cars, even though I rode my bicycle to work most days. I learned to drive in my dad's bright red 1967 Ford Mustang convertible. We would go to the parking lot of the high school and practice getting up enough speed so I could shift the manual gears. Finally, I fledged, and the first solo trip I can remember

David poses with his pickup truck outside his home at Selah, 2018.
Photo by Pam LeBlanc.

making delivered me to a drive-through hamburger joint a few miles away.

For nearly twenty years—spanning a time that I worked for a small newspaper in Plano, Texas, continuing to a seven-year stint at *The Monitor* in McAllen in South Texas and then at the *Austin American-Statesman*—I wrote car reviews. The last seven or eight years, I teamed with Pete Szilagyi, a former *Statesman* staffer who had retired, to pen the "Pete 'n Pam" column, in which he pontificated about the car's mechanics and I talked about what I did and did not like about the car. Cars. They are about way more than transportation.

~\|/~

My mother took the money she'd gotten from the settlement after my father died and bought a small farm out in the country, close to the shack we'd lived in before. Looking around the property, I found a 1927 Chevy with a rollback leather top, big wheels, and no spokes parked inside an old barn. I'd sit in that car and pretend I knew how to drive.

I don't remember why, but the man who sold us the property ended up giving me that old car. I was fourteen years old, and suddenly I had my own car—but I didn't have a driver's license. I did, however, have a plan. I sat down and wrote a letter to the governor of Ohio, pleading my case for a driver's license. I told him that my dad had been killed in an accident at a war plant, that my mother didn't know how to drive, that we lived in the country, that one of my older brothers was serving as a navigator in the US Air Force and the other was attending college in a different town as part of a US Navy program, that the nearest bus station was miles away and the bus only came by once a day.

I needed to drive, and he could help me. The governor wrote back, telling me to go to highway patrol headquarters. "If you can pass the test, ask them to give you a driver's license," he wrote. "Show them this letter." I took the test and got the license but was "officially" told I could use it only to drive my mom to the grocery store and back.

I wasn't too worried about that, but there was the problem of gas. About that time, my older brother Jim came home on leave. Ration stamps for gasoline were hard to come by, but soldiers could go to the ration board and get them when they took leave. Even better, Jim knew a girl on the ration board. Each stamp meant four gallons of gas. That girl Jim knew slipped him a handful of extra coupons. And when he left, he gave me a pack of those tickets. Suddenly I not only had a car but plenty of gas to run it. I was king. I drove that car, and not just to the grocery store with my mom. Hell, I drove it all over.

━╱╲━

Lessons from Mom

The stories started spilling out of David the first time I climbed into his pickup truck. For him, words flowed like water, something that was a constant source of conversation around Selah. At first, they trickled. After thirty seconds, and anybody who knows David will assure you that is about all the time it takes, they started pouring forth. After that, no kind of dam on the planet could hold them back. Plenty of those stories involved his mother.

We were heading out to the dig pit on the ranch one day, where we planned to spend the morning sifting through trenches, looking for chipped bits of flint and projectile points and other signs of people who lived on this land hundreds of years before we did. I did not know yet that he had a grand plan that involved me helping him write his stories, and I had yet to hear any of his classic tales about growing up poor in Ohio with no running water and no electricity. The thing about hearing David tell his stories firsthand was that you got to hear the inflection in his voice, the way he got excited and flapped his arms and then went all soft and dramatic, practically whispering parts of what he was saying.

David walks past Hes' Country Store, where many of his mother's possessions are displayed, late summer 2017. Photo by Rodolfo Gonzalez.

Some came with little skits, too, that he acted out or voices that he mimicked, trying to get the accent just right.

That was how it unfolded as we rattled along in his truck, unrolling the windows to let the dusty breeze ruffle the hair on our arms. When we approached Hes' Country Store, a landmark at Selah named for his mother Hester, who died in 1980, he started describing her. Pretty quickly I realized the impact she had had on his life. You could probably call me a daddy's girl. I am pretty sure David was a mama's boy. His love and respect for her came through with every word he spoke.

As he began to talk, I could picture the simple dresses Hester wore, her tiny stature, and the way she called her son Davy. Nearly every group that comes to visit Selah hears some of these same stories. Before they leave, they knew that Hes sent her boys out to gather greens and fruits that appeared on the family dinner table. They knew David tagged along when his mother planted trees and that years later, when he had moved to Texas, she still picked apples from trees that they planted together. They know that items from the house his mother lived in in Ohio are now

David sweeps the floor inside Hes' Country Store, where he often greets visitors and tells stories, summer 2017. Photo by Rodolfo Gonzalez.

displayed in the little country store at Selah. They know she gave him a copy of a book that to this day guides the work at the ranch. And they quickly learn she shaped his respect for other people, too.

~\|/~

Every bit of my love of nature came from my mother. She kept us outdoors and taught us about the birds and grasses and trees and wildlife. Early on, before we got running water at our house, we had to walk to the neighbor's house to get drinking water. Some days, my mother would hand us a colander and send us out to look for hazelnuts and berries along the way. She taught us which leaves and grasses to gather, and she'd make a salad with whatever we collected.

But my mom taught me about more than nature. She taught me respect, and I learned from her the right way to treat other people. During the war, hospitals desperately needed doctors and nurses. My mother had gone through a nursing program when she was in high school, and after my father and brother died, she took a job at the big state hospital along the highway in Massillon. At the same time, the hospital recruited medical workers from all over, and some came to our town from as far away as Mexico, Argentina, and the Philippines.

Mom embraced those workers. She'd invite them to bring their families out to our little farm in the country. We'd make a fire circle lined with stones and roast hot dogs and marshmallows. The kids would run all over the place. After a while, the hospital administrators heard about it. They didn't like it. They called my mother in and told her they knew what she was doing. "Mrs. Bamberger, it's been brought to our attention that you're socializing with these foreign doctors," they told her. "We don't do that."

She stared right back at them. "Maybe you don't, but I do," she said. That lesson stuck with me.

She also carried a commonsense attitude about health and wellness. One time, a woman came to the

David poses with a photo of his mother, Hester, at the country store at Selah, February 2017. Photo by Pam LeBlanc.

door carrying an empty quart jar. Mom disappeared down into the basement. She scooped up some of her homemade sauerkraut from a crock, filling that quart jar and handing it back to the woman. I don't know what she was treating that woman for, but Mom believed in vitamins and minerals and that whole you-are-what-you-eat philosophy.

When she got older, my mother developed arthritis. She went to the Cleveland Clinic for treatment, and doctors there wanted to put her on steroids. My mother refused. Instead, she turned to a book about arthritis and how to treat it naturally. Because of that book, she took so much cod liver oil and garlic that it oozed through her skin.

People came to her all the time for help. They'd knock on her door, describe their ailment, and ask for her advice. One winter day when six or eight inches of snow had fallen, she heard a rap at the door. She swung it open and found herself looking at a guy standing there smoking a cigarette.

"Mrs. Bamberger, please, I need your advice," he started.

She stopped him right there. "If you don't quit that damn smoking, you're going to be sicker yet," she told him. Then she closed the door.

Other people recognized it, too. When I buried my mother, this man with a big belly came up to me after the service. He lived out at the crossroads near where my mom had lived, and he owned a Jeep with a blade on it. Every time it snowed, people called him up and asked him to clear the road. One day, he told me, after a big snow had fallen, making big white mounds that nobody could drive through, he headed out in his Jeep. He came down the road and saw a little figure moving off in the distance. When he finally caught up, he realized it was my mother, marching along in the snow.

He slowed down to talk to her, but she didn't stop moving. He pulled up ahead of her and said, "Mrs. Bamberger, get over here in my Jeep. You shouldn't be out here walking like this."

My mom put her hand on his belly and looked him straight in the face. "I shouldn't, but you sure should," she told him.

Right after my mom died, I got the nicest letter from a woman. "Mr. B, you don't know me, but Hilda Deal was my mother," the letter said. My mom had respected and admired Hilda, who had raised nine children. "I was eighteen and got pregnant," the letter said. "Your mother came to my aid. She talked to me about how to prepare and what would happen, and she was never critical. All my friends and the community shunned me where I lived. There was nobody except your mother."

That's what she taught me. That it doesn't matter what anybody else thinks, that you do the right thing.

2

The Door-to-Door Days

David met his high school sweetheart, Donna Beem, while canoeing across a small lake near Akron during the summer of 1944. Donna had gone to the lake with an older neighbor girl and some other friends and was paddling across the glimmering pond when David and another boy canoed past. She was smitten; he was too. He enrolled at Navarre High School so he could court her.

David's moneymaking schemes were maturing at about the same time. Instead of gathering and selling berries, he began collecting and fixing used bicycles, then repairing used cars. Just after graduating from high school, he enlisted in the US Army, where he became an information and education specialist, training recruits how to spin military news in a way that meshed with the government's goals. Considering David's mastery of storytelling and embellishing, the job sounded like a perfect fit. He did not exactly thrive under the authoritarian principles of his job, though, and wound up spending a lot of time on kitchen duty.

David tells funny stories about those years. He worked part-time at a military golf course on the base and used some of that time to fish misfired golf balls out of ponds and sand traps. He sold those balls for fifty cents each and once caught the wrath of

David recalls stories from his early days while sitting in his workroom, April 2016. Photo by Pam LeBlanc.

an officer who spotted his initials on one of the reclaimed balls. When the officer demanded it back, David stood up to his superior, telling the man the wayward golf ball was now his to sell since he had fished it out of the water. That did not sit well, and David won more time on kitchen duty, picking gravel out of dry beans that fed the soldiers. He adopted the same priorities when it came to love. In 1947, he went AWOL—sneaking away for a few days to marry Donna. Somehow he managed to avoid serious punishment for that disappearance.

David eventually got promoted, and part of his work included running a high school equivalency program for fellow recruits. He also took college extension courses, earning advance university credit. After an eighteen-month stint in the US Army, David enrolled at Kent State University. Benefits he earned through the GI Bill paid for tuition and books, plus a monthly subsistence check of $125. "The army experience was good for me—and to me," he said.

When the couple's first son, David, was born in 1949, though, David needed more money to support his growing family. When he happened to meet a vacuum cleaner salesman who told him about his success selling door-to-door, David wondered if it might work for him. Not everyone thought so highly of the plan. Door-to-door salesmen did not exactly rise to the top of any list of best jobs in America, and few people would claim that someone who walked from home to home, trying to convince residents that they needed an electric sweeper to make life easier, was reaching the epitome of his or her potential.

Still, David saw the advantages. "I could pick my own hours, be my own boss." He decided to try it. He signed up, loaded some vacuum cleaners into his car, practiced his sales pitch, and began knocking on doors. Fairly quickly, he started earning decent money through "direct selling," the preferred term among those who were recruiting others to sell door-to-door. At the time, David commuted about forty miles to the university. Every day after

David sorts through papers, newspaper clippings, and magazine articles in his workroom, April 2016. Photo by Pam LeBlanc.

class, he knocked on doors on his way back from classes, making a note of which houses had nobody home so he could come back to them later and try again.

Anybody Need a B-29?

Selling vacuum cleaners door-to-door could get tricky at times, as David learned. When he made cold calls at homes, he never knew who would answer the door, what situation he might walk into, or who might come barreling in the door once he had made a sale. Lucky for David, he never landed in a situation he could not wrangle his way out of, like this one, one of his favorites.

⁓

Every time I made a sale, I'd tell my customers that if they made a referral that brought me another sale, I'd give them ten dollars. They had incentive, and a lot of times those referrals were easy money. Early on, I got a lead from one of my customers. I made a phone call and set up an appointment so I could show her the vacuum cleaner. The woman I called on lived in an upstairs apartment in a big old house. The demonstration went well, and the woman liked the product and wanted to buy the vacuum cleaner. She signed the contract, and just like that, I got another sale.

Once that was settled, I needed to show her how to use the thing. So I got down on the floor with her and started pointing out different attachments and how to make them work, when we heard a commotion. I heard a series of thuds—someone was racing up the stairs. With a grunt, a burly man burst through the door, shouting at us.

"What's going on here?" he wanted to know.

She smiled at him and said, "I'm buying myself a vacuum cleaner."

Me, I was shivering in my shoes. This big bruiser of a guy obviously had flown into a rage. He was mad, perhaps suspicious, and here I was, a young man crawling around on the floor with his charming wife.

"You need a vacuum cleaner like I need a B-29," he yelled at her.

She stayed just as calm and cool as a dead fish in an ice chest. "You just go ahead and buy your B-29," she told him. "I'm buying myself this vacuum cleaner."

Only the person who did my laundry knew how scared I was.

✧

Paying with a Cashier's Check

David and Donna moved to Texas in 1950, where he continued selling vacuum cleaners from his new home base in San Antonio. He never exactly loved the work, but he had found something he was good at and that helped support his family. After he reached a certain level of success as a salesman, he no longer banged on doors himself to peddle the product. He supervised a team of agents who did that work for him. Those years, he often says, taught him more than he ever learned at the university.

"Hey, for seventeen years I sold vacuum cleaners," he says. "I liked the money I was making, but I didn't like the work. I walked away from many houses where someone said, 'Bamberger, if anybody told me I was going to buy a vacuum cleaner today, I'd have told them they were nuts.' What they bought from me was a lot of hyperbole. You can take a broom and romance it."

It is easy to understand why David did well at the work. He puts you at ease. He seems like the guy who grew up down the street. His trusty dog tags along everywhere he goes, he loves to joke with people, and he is quick to laugh.

"Knocking on doors to make a living wasn't the easiest thing to do, but it taught me so much," he said. "The most valuable thing I learned was how to handle rejection, and just as importantly, how to smile and stay enthused no matter the case."

He met all kinds of people, from doctors and educators to business owners, factory workers, and military personnel, all with their own unique life experiences. He also learned a thing or two about how to make sure people treated him fairly and how to apply pressure at just the right time to make things happen. "I learned that in every block in any town or any neighborhood there were heartache and discontent. It could be financial, health related, marital, family, alcohol, or drugs—all manner of things. But along the way, there were so many laughs, so many stories."

~\⁄⁄~

In the mid-1950s, we'd load up our cars with vacuum cleaners, all neatly packaged, and fan out to the small towns around San Antonio to sell our goods. Sometimes we'd head one hundred miles out and stay out for a whole week at a time. I always told the salespeople, "If you sell a vacuum cleaner for cash and get a check, take the check to the bank and get a cashier's check." Back then, the Kirby vacuum cleaner sold for $157.40, and that was a hell of a lot of money.

One day one of my employees sold a Kirby to a woman. A few days later, he went back to visit her and to make sure she was happy with her purchase and knew how to use it. Everything was working just fine for her. When the salesman returned to our office, he turned in all his orders, including a cashier's check for the one he'd sold to that woman. I made my bank deposit, and a day later got a call from the bank saying that the woman's check for $157.40 wasn't any good.

I said, "That was a cashier's check, and cashier's checks are guaranteed by the bank."

Even so, the guy on the phone told me that that particular check had been canceled at the request of the president of the bank in her small town. That's just not right. At the sales meeting that day, I invited the crew to join me in a little demonstration of activism. We painted up some signs that said "bank fraud," and we drove downtown—eight of us—and started marching around the bank building, chanting, "Unfair, Bexar Bank, unfair."

That roused some of the bank officials pretty quickly. They wanted to know what was going on. Pretty soon, the bank president came out. He spotted me and my men moving around on the sidewalk. The police showed up, and they couldn't do anything, because we were legally there, on the sidewalk. The bank president asked me why we were marching. I told him it was because he'd stolen $157.40 that belonged to me. He promised to reimburse me, if we'd all get back into our cars and disappear. And that's what happened. I got my money back, and we left.

What I found out later was that the woman's husband had come home after work and found out that his wife had spent money on a vacuum cleaner. He didn't want her spending money on the sweeper. He wanted to stop payment, but he couldn't, because it was a cashier's check. But he knew the bank president, who took care of it for him. At least temporarily.

--》｜〈--

Words with Khrushchev

In the 1950s and 1960s, when the Cold War had amped up tensions between the United States and the Soviet Union, David's workforce included a particularly memorable woman from Russia who could sling cuss words as well as anyone in Bexar County. A top seller, Maria did not mince words. David admired her style.

In 1959, Nikita Khrushchev became the first Soviet premier to visit the United States. He was "curious to have a look at America," according to PBS's *The American Experience*, and leaders from both countries hoped the visit would help thaw the Cold War chill. The White House, under President Dwight Eisenhower, issued an invitation, and planners sketched out an itinerary that included visits to Washington, DC; New York; California; Iowa; and Pennsylvania.

On the tour route? A trip to a meatpacking plant, where Khrushchev reportedly announced, "We have beaten you to the moon, but you have beaten us in sausage making." He also stopped by an agricultural experiment station in Maryland, where he supposedly complained that the pigs were too fat and the turkeys too small. No word on what he thought of Maria Pults, the feisty saleswoman who worked with David and who managed to meet the premier in person while he was in America. Before Khrushchev's trip ended, she had become a sizzling power line, spewing sparks of four-letter words, and he and his entourage were dry grass, going up in flames in her wake.

~\\/~

In the mid-1950s, I hired a woman named Maria Pults from Russia. She grew up in Kiev and told me that she couldn't count how many times she'd been raped by Germans during World War II. She spoke broken English, but boy could she swear. Every word she uttered would make you blush. She and her husband, a mechanic for Braniff Airlines, had three children, but her mother and the rest of her family still lived in Kiev. She'd been trying to move her mother to the United States for years but couldn't get through to anyone in Russia who could help her.

You could describe her as bold and brash and forward, but she and another salesman I had were the top salespeople in the country, at least twice. She knew how to get people to pay attention to her. One day she read in a newspaper that Khrushchev planned to visit the United States to tour pig farms. She watched him on television, speaking at the United Nations. He whipped off one shoe and slapped it against the lectern to make a point. Now he was coming to a pig farm just a few states away.

You can imagine the security that accompanied a visit like that, but Maria said to me, "God damn, Dave. I'm going up there." And I've got news for you; she did. Maria flew out of San Antonio for free, because her husband worked for the airline. She somehow found her way out to that farm, and when she got there, she met swarms of Russian guards and American security forces. That didn't matter. You had to know Maria. She pushed her way through the American guards, even though they tried to restrain her. She said in Russian, "Tell these sons of bitches to leave me alone."

Eventually she got up to Khrushchev, who was inspecting those fat pigs. "Look at me, you son of a bitch," she ordered him in her native tongue. "I've been trying to get my mother over here for years, and no one in the government will answer my letters."

Khrushchev couldn't believe it. Who was this woman, and why was she cussing at him? He told her to write down all the pertinent information about her family members and give it to his assistant. She did. A photograph of her confronting Khrushchev even appeared in *Life* magazine. I'm not sure what else she said to the Russian leader, but it must have made an impression. And you know what? Maria got her mother over here.

Helping Fay Buy a House

In the 1950s and 1960s, as David built his vacuum cleaner sales business and later his chicken chain, he saw firsthand discrimination against African Americans as well as Mexican Americans, and the topic comes up over and over again when he recounts stories of the people who worked with him. He wanted his employees treated fairly, whether it was on the job as a door-to-door sweeper salespeople, at work at Church's, or on the ranch. And when that did not happen, he sometimes went out of his way to make things right. Or at least that is how he tells the story.

A salesman named Fay Williams worked for me in the 1960s. He drove a very nice automobile, married a beautiful woman, charmed everyone with his clean-cut good looks, and climbed to the top of my sales force. He also happened to be black. At first, he worked selling vacuum cleaners mainly in black neighborhoods. I sent him on appointments in white neighborhoods, but because of the times and the discrimination, he faced challenges. Still, he worked hard at it.

Fay and his wife wanted to buy a new house, and they found one for sale in an all-white neighborhood in San Antonio. Back then, though, they couldn't find a real estate agent willing to help them buy it. As soon as one of them saw the color of Fay's skin, they turned him away. He came to me for advice, and I told him I'd try to help.

He drove me out to Montfort Street in San Antonio, an upper-middle-class neighborhood off San Pedro Avenue where no Hispanics or blacks lived at the time, to show me a house that had caught his eye. Fay jotted down the phone number of a realtor, and I went back to my shop and called the woman up. I told her my wife and I were moving to San Antonio and we'd been shopping around for a place to live. "I see you've got a house out here, and I'd like to look at it real quick," I said.

We set up an appointment. Now here's where it gets sneaky. Three of my Kirby salesmen agreed to go with me. While I was busy distracting the realtor, they'd sneak into every room in the house and unlock the windows. Later that night Fay, his wife, and I returned to the house with flashlights. We checked it out, toured it like it was on the Parade of Homes, and they just loved it. You could feel happiness flood over them as we drove off.

The next day, I called the realtor back and told her my wife was due to have a baby in a couple of days, and I might surprise her with the house. I just needed a little time to think about it. I had a little religion in my blood at the time, and I happened to be involved with a church. A guy in my Sunday school class, a lawyer, agreed to help me out, even though he didn't approve of my plan. Still, he drew up an earnest money contract for me, and I had him put "J. David Bamberger or assigns" on it, which meant that it applied to me or anyone else I assigned to it. Back at my office, I called the realtor again. "I'm just going to go ahead and buy it," I told her.

But I made a big mistake. I'm like that. I just bust in and do stuff. And this time, I didn't say anything to Donna, my wife, about what I was doing. Three weeks later, when the contract got to the title company, I called and told them I'd like to assign my title contract to Fay and his wife, Gladys. It all went through, and here comes Fay, black as an ace of spades, into that neighborhood. Then all hell broke loose. The neighbors figured out what had happened, and they teamed up and put me and Donna on their call list. They rang us twenty-four hours a day, calling us "nigger-loving bastards."

Fay stood strong. He still moved in. At first, the neighbors huffed and puffed and dumped junk in his front yard. Within a year, though, feelings shifted. Fay and Gladys had organized more block parties and backyard barbecues than anyone else. They slowly made friends. The neighbors grew to appreciate them.

Later on, when I had finished with the vacuum business and Bill Church and I were starting our chicken business, we wrote a list of principles that would guide how we worked together. We agreed that so long as we were red-blooded, flag-waving, apple pie–eating Americans, race would never affect our business—or our working relationships.

One day, Bill called me into his office. It turned out we had a real estate man who lived on the same street where Fay lived. He'd come in and told Bill, "The damnedest thing has happened. The National Association for the Advancement of Colored People has made an effort to integrate our neighborhood." Bill laughed. None of that is true, he said. The black family that had moved in were friends of David's, Bill told him, and David was the one who helped him get that house.

—)⁄¹∖⁄—

3

The World of Fried Chicken

At times David's life seems like the lives of three or four men, merged into one. Some parts of it he is more open to sharing than others. He will tell you all about his childhood, especially his mother, and a little about his vacuum cleaner days, mainly because of the lessons he learned at those times in his life. He would rather slide right past the Church's part, it seems, sizzling it off like scrap bits of batter in a big boiling vat of oil, to get on to what is really meaningful to him—his work healing the land and teaching other people to do the same. But for a few days, I managed to pin him down, practically by force, and make him tell me about the fried-chicken business and everything that went along with it.

Getting Started with Church's

David met Bill Church, his future business partner, by happenstance. Bill was hauling a bag filled with paint and brushes down city streets in San Antonio one cool fall afternoon, making a little money by freehand painting holiday decorations on storefront windows. He knocked on the door of the office where David headquartered his vacuum cleaner sales business, and David let him

David poses in front of a Church's fried-chicken restaurant in San Antonio, December 2017. Photo by Pam LeBlanc.

go to work with his paintbrushes, brightening two big plate-glass windows with a Christmas message.

The two started talking, with no idea then that a fast-food empire loomed in their mutual future. They chatted for a while, and a friendship developed. Bill needed work. David could use more people out there peddling Kirby sweepers. Bill joined the door-to-door sales force. "It wasn't big volume, but he had wonderful composure and a big smile," said David, sorting through boxes of crunchy, yellowed newspaper clippings in his workroom at Selah, looking for evidence to corroborate some of these memories.

Bill's father, David said, had once worked at a chicken-processing facility near Waco for the Youngblood's group of restaurants, in the days long before drive-through fast-food restaurants doled out hamburgers, french fries, and soft-serve ice-cream cones on every other city street corner. In those days, only a few McDonald's were serving the burger-hungry public, and Woolworth's, a dime store with a lunch counter inside, ranked as the biggest restaurant chain in America. Youngblood's, which operated a restaurant in downtown San Antonio, boasted a dining room as big as "two tennis courts pushed together," David told me, admitting that he was possibly stretching the truth a tad. Customers came to see the giant ball of twine that the restaurant used to tie up the

The first Church's restauants were drive-ups, with no indoor seating. Courtesy David Bamberger.

raw poultry as much as they came to enjoy a Sunday-afternoon meal of fried chicken.

Bill's father eventually left the Youngblood's processing plant in Waco and moved to San Antonio, where he opened three tiny chicken stores of his own on plots of land so small they were not much good for anything else. (David later wrote an essay about the elder Church, calling him "America's Fast Food Prophet.") Every square inch counted in those three original stores. Customers never actually went inside the four hundred–square-foot structures. They parked their cars, walked up to the pint-sized buildings, and ordered their chicken, fries, and Cokes at a pass-through window. The stores plugged modestly along, but nobody was getting rich.

When the senior Church died, Bill's older brother Bob stepped in to help his mother manage the stores. While Bill stayed busy selling Kirby sweepers with David, Bob gradually expanded the family business to nine modest chicken stores. But after a few years, Bob left the family business. The rest of the Church family turned to Bill to take over the chicken stores. Bill turned in his dirt-sucking sweepers and bid goodbye to David.

David, in the meantime, carried on, supervising a team of door-to-door salesmen (and a few women) who armed housekeepers in the greater San Antonio area with the dirt-slurping machines they needed to keep dust at bay. Bill, though, did not stay away long. About a year after he left the vacuum business, he returned to David's vacuum sales office one day, hanging around until most of the other salespeople had left for the day to work their territories. "I thought he was just chatting and thinking about coming back," said David.

But Bill had more on his mind. He needed a loan for one thousand dollars to pay his employees at the chicken stores. "I said, 'Bill, when I was at the university, I had a hard time passing accounting. But I know this: If you have a business without enough money to make payroll, you don't have much of a business.'"

David wanted to help financially, but he was building a new house of his own at the time and had three young children to support. He had no business loaning anybody any money. Bill explained to David that his chicken stores were making money, but he was trying to improve the way things worked. He had spent all the profits on research and development, trying to replicate something he had seen while he served in the navy—pumps that moved hydraulic oil through machinery, filtering it and reusing it.

The problem with frying chicken in vast quantities in those days came in keeping the oil fresh and clean. After sizzling up a few batches of chicken and fries, the oil would turn cloudy with bits and pieces of flour and batter. Food cooked in used oil just did not taste as good. It had to be replaced periodically with a fresh supply of oil to keep the product at its best. Bill wanted to develop a filter that would apply the same premise used in the navy's pump system to the shortening used in a chicken fryer. That would save money, because other than chicken, shortening was the most expensive part of making fried chicken. In the end, David loaned Bill the money, with the promise that Bill would repay him within a month.

A month went by after I made the loan to Bill. Then another. I started to wonder about the loan I'd made. Should I hassle Bill a little bit to get my money back? Before I could get around to it, Bill strolled back into my office on West Hildebrand Street at the end of the workday one afternoon. Some of the other salespeople teased him as he walked in the door, calling out, "Churchy, bring us some chicken." I thought he'd finally come back to settle his debt. I thought, oh man, he's going to pay me my thousand dollars. But that's not why Bill had returned. He still hadn't solved the oil filter problem, and he wanted me to loan him another thousand dollars to figure it out.

One of my salesmen, a man name Otis, overheard the conversation and asked Bill if he'd ever traded in an Electrolux brand of sweeper. This tank-type vacuum cleaner filtered dirt into a compartment that had to be emptied periodically. Otis suggested that Bill make the chicken fryer's oil filter just like the Electrolux, with a "bag" that could handle heat and oil that would then be pumped back into the fryer. Bill tucked the idea away in his mind. It might just work.

I gave Bill a second loan that day, but this time I added a caveat. I'd give Bill the loan if in addition to the thousand dollars I'd get an equity kicker—a thousand shares of the fledgling fried-chicken company's stock, to be delivered as ten certificates worth one hundred shares each. That way, I could give them as sales-incentive prizes to my Kirby sweeper sales crew. We made a deal.

But again, a week, two weeks, three weeks, and then seven weeks passed and Bill didn't bring me the stock certificates. I climbed into my car and drove to the Church's office, which was located inside a crowded warehouse stacked high with bags of flour, drums of shortening, and pallets of paper bags ready for distribution to the chicken stores. When I got there, I couldn't find Bill, but I found his sister, who was working as the office manager. I told her about the deal Bill and I had made and told her I hadn't gotten the certificates for shares of the company. She looked at me hard, then told me they didn't even have enough money to buy blank certificates. I thought, "Oh my God." I turned around and left.

⌐ヽ|ヽ⌐

The Continuous Filter Fryer

Bill finally did come up with a continuous filter fryer system to cook chicken based on the idea of the Electrolux vacuum that David's employee had suggested. He cut the bottom out of a fryer to make room for a drainpipe. He used copper piping at first but quickly realized that a chemical reaction with copper caused the shortening to break down. He switched to iron, and the system worked. The key to the new fryer was a stainless-steel mesh filter bag and a dash of diatomaceous earth that was stirred into the oil

David loads boxes of chicken into the company van in this undated photo. Courtesy David Bamberger.

in the fryer. That held the particles—crispy bits of chicken batter and fried potatoes—together and kept them from going back into the fryer where fresh chicken was cooked.

"That's the way the filter was developed," David told me there in his workroom at Selah, like he was explaining the moral of a Dr. Seuss made-for-TV holiday special. "The only difference was you're not sucking dirt; you're sucking hot oil."

That changed everything for the young startup chicken company. Bill began installing the redesigned fryer at his nine walkup chicken stores, and sales started climbing. Not only did the new equipment save money on shortening, because crews did not have to replace it so often, but using it to cook made the chicken taste better because the oil was cleaner.

"You didn't get a piece of greasy-ass chicken," David said, laughing like everyone knew that would be the absolute worst thing that could happen to anyone. "And it was two pieces for forty-nine cents—and they were big pieces."

Other reasons played into the store's success, of course. David says Church's cut a 2.75-pound chicken into eight pieces, but the competition cut smaller chickens into nine pieces. David began to notice that this fried-chicken business just might be worth investigating a little more closely. "I thought, God, what an opportunity this is for me."

Not long afterward, he picked up a book called *The Franchise Boom* by Harry Kursh that made a difference in what happened next. It described the growing popularity of franchising and spelled out how individuals could go into business for themselves by affiliating with a larger, established company. That way, the company could also expand quickly. David became convinced that the franchising idea would work with the Church's model. He also knew that he was growing tired, after seventeen years of promoting door-to-door sales, of the vacuum business.

He called Bill and told him he needed to see him that day. Bill agreed. When they sat down, David handed his future partner a copy of the book and asked him to read it. "I get the book in his hands, and he, too, reads it in one or two days and calls me," David said.

The book did not focus on restaurants in particular, but David and Bill believed its concepts of business identity and efficient service would apply to chicken restaurants. "I said, 'Bill, if you can make those stores conform to this guy's deal, I can sell franchises and we can expand this company.'" The two men talked philosophy. "At that stage of my life, I was a big ass, rightwing Republican, supporting Barry Goldwater," David says. (He is certainly not that today.) So was Bill. "I remember Bill and I sitting down and writing out our philosophy, that we believed in capitalism and all of these things, and we asked our suppliers to sign on to it, too."

But the two men disagreed on one point: minimum wage. In the late 1960s, restaurants were exempt from the federal minimum-wage requirement. Bill, like his father before him, believed that if minimum-wage legislation passed, their chicken restaurants would fail. David disagreed. He explained this to me in colorful, expletive-filled language, which is the way most of his stories come out—like perfectly golden-colored biscuits, with slightly crusty edges.

"That's bullshit," he said. "You think if you've got a successful business and minimum wage goes up ten or fifteen cents it's going to shut you down? No. You pass part of it down to your customers. I told him minimum wage was something we needed to think about." But Bill would not budge. "On that issue, I had no voice," David says.

Even so, David decided to invest in the new company they would form called Church's Food Service Industries. The company would continue operating the nine fried-chicken stores the Church family owned in San Antonio in exchange for exclusive rights to open Church's fried-chicken restaurants elsewhere in the world. David spent about a year learning the ropes alongside Bill while simultaneously maintaining the vacuum business. "I never intended to peddle vacuum cleaners door-to-door for seventeen years," he said. But he had made good money at it and did not want to give it up until he knew the fried-chicken business held a future for him.

The business needed an injection of money, too. At the time, Bob Church, Bill's brother, had opened a franchise store in Fort

Worth. For personal reasons, he needed to sell the store and lease it back. Bob offered to pay a "triple net lease," one that let him pay the rent, maintenance, and taxes while the investor earned 12 percent on his money. David was game but did not have enough money to buy a store building outright. He signed a bank loan and made the deal. Suddenly, a check arrived in his mailbox every month. The arrangement worked so well that Bob opened two new franchises in Fort Worth, and David financed them. Now David owned three Church's buildings—not the businesses but the brick-and-mortar structures. He spent time in North Texas, learning how to operate them smoothly, and when he came back to San Antonio, he officially left the vacuum business and clocked his first week as a fulltime member of Church's Food Service Industries management. He was just in his thirties.

"My job was humans—everything from the uniforms they wore, to how to tie a tie, everything," he said.

David had learned a lot from his time in the door-to-door business, when he "hired" people on straight commission. He had sold to rich people, poor people, intellectuals, salt-of-the-earth types, people who lived in huge mansions, and people who lived in shacks. Now he wanted to bring what he had learned to the fried-chicken business. He liked repeating the old saying, "The only place that success comes before work is in the dictionary." (He liked other sayings, too, like "Never initiate an action you're unable to sustain" and "Don't start something you can't finish.")

The new company would manage the existing nine chicken stores the Church family owned in San Antonio, the four hundred–square-foot kind with no indoor seating or drive-throughs. They sold hot fried chicken, french fries, soft drinks, jalapeño peppers, and, early on, scratch-made pies—peach, cherry, and apple, shaped like a half moon, baked in their own ovens. A lot of work stood in front of them. Bill handled in-house construction. David, whose downhome, easygoing way swayed people toward him, hired the workers and made sure they were trained in every aspect of store operations.

"I was so proud of our young startup company," David said. He could finally offer a "real job" to people answering his ads. But not everybody wants to go to school just to flip burgers or make pizza, and he knew that. "They go to school so they don't have to work at Jack in the Box," he said. David wanted to help the men and women he hired to earn more income—and Church's to earn more profit—through incentive-based programs. It had worked in the sweeper business, so why wouldn't it work now?

As David molded his role at the company, he started a policy of hiring those who had not had the opportunity to attend college or were forced, by life's circumstance, to make do with less than others. He wanted to nurture confidence in the people he hired and teach them to become more productive, valuable employees. He wanted to help them turn their lives around—and he realized that if they did, they could in turn make his business profitable. "Because of our success, we were expanding rapidly, making opportunities for everyone to move up into managerial positions and beyond," he said.

At the main Church's office in San Antonio, David gathered the managers of the local Church's stores for a weekly meeting. He wanted to share some of the skills he had learned selling vacuum cleaners with them. "Door-to-door selling is not a slam dunk," he told me. "You have to be able to handle rejection when people don't let you into their home." To motivate his staff, he indulged in a little of his trademark tent-revival preacher artistry. "I saw so much opportunity to increase sales by bringing in some new thinking—primarily by introducing simple changes, changes that these nine men would make if only it were introduced in a friendly way. I never believed in dictating to the men (and women) I recruited to sell Kirbys, and I wouldn't do that here."

He started with some personal hygiene tips, which he thought might come in handy for employees who had to work in hot, cramped conditions. Back then, the Church's stores had no central air-conditioning, just an evaporative cooler on the roof that pumped air into the store. When the slider window opened, air rushed out. When customers walked up to order a box of chicken, David wanted them to smell hot fried chicken, not sweaty workers. At one of those managerial meetings, he pulled out a stick of Old Spice deodorant. He passed it around, so everyone could get a whiff. They all chuckled.

"What is it?" David asked. It smelled like perfume, someone called out. That perfume, David said, was better than what customers sometimes got when they placed an order. He installed a shower stall from Sears and Roebuck at the warehouse where managers met before heading to their respective stores. He suggested that those who spent time working on their cars clean under their fingernails.

David also invited his employees to share their own ideas about improving the stores. "They had truly become part of something bigger—'Hey, we're managers!'" David said.

Just one problem persisted: getting chicken and supplies to those compact restaurants, which did not have enough room to store much. In San Antonio, where those first Church's stores operated, a truck delivered chicken, flour, and shortening to each location every day. Bill came up with the idea for a single-unit store, each complete with its own storage space. Each store manager would be responsible for ordering his or her own supplies, as needed.

Church's reach spread, and as the company grew, David began to hire managers to operate the new restaurants. He traveled around the state, tracking down store managers he thought would help Church's succeed. He did not look for college graduates; he looked for people who wanted opportunity and had what he called "command presence." He arranged a trip to South Texas, set up a temporary office in a Holiday Inn, and spread the word via business cards, notices at stores, and newspaper advertisements that he was hiring. Then he brought in large groups of potential employees to interview. Nothing in any of the ads mentioned what kind of job he was offering.

"I'd start out and say, 'I'd like to think this is a great day for you. I know it is for me. But I do know something. Everybody is in this room because either you don't have a job, the job you have is not satisfactory, or you've been laid off because it's raining and that means you can't do construction work. I'm here to tell you none of those things will ever happen again if you work with my company. It doesn't matter if it's raining, cold, or snowing. You'll always have a job, every day," he told his roomful of potential Rio Grande Valley recruits.

When David found the right people to run the stores, he sent them to San Antonio, where he had set up a Church's training school in a pair of houses on Hackberry Avenue. One served as a dorm, so the company did not have to put up workers in a hotel; the other, a real store, where employees learned how to cut up chicken, fry it, open the store every day, and clean up after hours.

Students even learned some basic chemistry applicable to the fried-chicken business. For example, heat, air, and certain metals, like copper, wreak havoc on shortening. And Church's bought a lot of shortening. To demonstrate, instructors would drop a copper penny into a few gallons of hot oil. The oil started foaming, evidence that the oil was breaking down. Then they would reverse the process by removing the penny and dropping in a silver dime.

Putting the Gorilla to Work

In those early years, David drew from his door-to-door days often. He remembered how he had organized contests, taught new salespeople to make calls, and incorporated families into the organization. He did not have a big media budget to advertise through television or radio, and it was not much use advertising just one store at a time anyway. He relied mostly on door-to-door visits and handbills—and a little free-chicken-fueled persuasion. "I was excited. I worked unbelievable hours each week. I didn't have anything to do while opening a new store in some other city but work," he said.

The week before a store opened, David and other employees put on their Church's uniforms—white shirt, tie, and a little paper hat with the Church's name on it. They walked the streets in the neighborhoods surrounding the new restaurant, knocking on doors and handing out gift cards for free chicken to be redeemed on opening day. That built goodwill, and people who drove by when the store opened would see a line of customers and think, "Wow! Look at that line. It must be good."

David did not stop there. The night before a store opened, he threw a party for employees and their families, serving fried chicken and soda. Spouses, kids, and parents all saw that this was a good company to work for, and the new workers got the message that the company cared.

—⋰—

We used incentives and contests to motivate workers. Workers could climb their way up the company ladder by selling more chicken and sides like fries, jalapeño peppers, and Coke. Take the Twelve Steps for Success plan that I unveiled at a staff meeting one morning. I asked the managers how many of them would do everything I suggested if it guaranteed them a raise every week and there was nothing illegal about it. Every hand shot up.

"We're going to start something, and you're part of it, but you have to trust me and do everything I ask you to do," I told them. Then I explained that each store would get its own "gorilla."

"What the heck is a gorilla?" they asked me.

"That's the amount of sales your store would get

David in the early Church's days. Courtesy David Bamberger.

each day if we replaced you with a gorilla," I said. They laughed. That was a good sign. The gorilla represented the store's sales for the previous month. "But you can do better than a gorilla," I told them. "And we'll reward you for that."

At first, managers would earn a set amount of money per pay period. Under the gorilla plan, each week they'd get a percentage raise based on how much over their gorilla the store brought in. Later, they would also earn a percentage—up to 8 percent—of their store's profit. That encouraged workers to control costs along with raising sales.

Then I dropped the kicker, Step 13, and it was big. At this point, a successful store manager could join a program that led to ownership of a store. But to get it, the employee had to set up a special bank account at Frost Bank and divert the profit sharing to that account. He couldn't spend that money on just anything. He had to save it. The program was meant to encourage the store managers to exercise personal discipline with how they spent money.

The Church's board of directors didn't always agree my ideas, and this was one of those times. "You're giving the company away," they told me when they first heard about the gorilla program. Even Bill questioned the method. But I believed that now that we had the fryers working and had lowered flour and oil expenditures, and sales were going up each week, we could pass some of the company profits on to the employees.

We had other programs, too. Qualifying store managers could load up a cart at a supermarket with as many groceries as they could in half an hour. Through another contest, winners earned appliances, school supplies, and clothing from Walmart. Church's got free publicity for the stunts, too. I knew how to motivate people in the store to make sure the windows were cleaner and that there weren't flies flying around. I knew how to make sure they would say, "Hey, what are you going to have today?"

It worked. Once, it worked so well that the father of one of our store managers almost didn't believe it. A store manager in McAllen named Tommy called me one night, asking for help. Tommy's family was planning a family reunion, and everyone was pitching in to buy supplies. Tommy offered to pay for the beer.

"I can afford it; I make twelve thousand dollars a year," Tommy told his father. But Tommy's father didn't believe him. For years, the family had driven to the Midwest every summer, where they worked picking produce. He called Tommy a liar and said no Mexican in the United States could earn as much money as he made in a single year. Tommy asked me to call his father to let him know that he really did make twelve thousand dollars a year and could afford to buy the beer.

⁓⁄\⁓

The Streets of Laredo

When Bill and David decided to add more stores, they hand-picked the cities where the company would expand. Not that they always relied on statistical data to make those decisions. Sometimes they just left it to chance—or, in one case, a book. That kept things fun and led them to places they might not otherwise have gone. As it turned out, that idea worked pretty well.

⁓\⁄⁓

Other companies spend hundreds of thousands of dollars on research for site selection. Ours was simple. We ended up picking up a book about Texas cities. I said to Bill, "You pick a page number, and I'll pick a row number." Then we flipped to the designated page in the book and counted down the designated number of rows. That determined where we'd put our first single-unit store.

We wind up with Laredo. A few weeks later, we head down there and spend an entire day driving up and down city streets. Back then, only a few of the streets were paved. Through all that driving, I don't see it, but Bill looked at neighborhoods and contemplated access. Then, after he made all the internal calculations, he figured it out.

"Really, we ought to be right there on Guadalupe Street," he tells me. I stop the car. Look out the window. See nothing but a worn-out house and a heavyset Hispanic guy up there on the porch with three or four little kids running around the dried-up yard.

"There's no lot there," I say. But Bill is certain. This is the spot. It's a busy street, and cars are whizzing past. We sit there for a minute; then I decide to go for it. What the heck. We'd picked this city randomly. What did we have to lose? I say, "Chief, let me go up and have a crack at this guy." Bill settles down for a nap in the car while I walk up to the house and introduce myself to the man sitting on the front porch.

"Me and my buddy want to put a fried-chicken store

David poses with stacks of fried-chicken boxes in this undated photo. Courtesy David Bamberger.

in Laredo, and we'd like it to be on Guadalupe Street,"
I tell him. "And you probably want to get off this busy
street with all these kids of yours." The man listens. He
tells me he already owns another lot, a few blocks away,
but he can't afford to build a house on it. We walk over to
take a look. Then I go out on a limb. I tell him we'll move
the house he's living in over a few blocks to the other lot.
Not only that, we'll pay him another five or six thousand dollars on top of it to help with the move, a decent
amount back then.

We shake hands, and I've bought the place for our
chicken store. In all, I'm gone maybe a couple of hours. I
go back to the car and find Bill still asleep. I wake him up
and tell him what I've done. He can't believe it, but it's
true. He later arranges to send someone down to move
the man's house over to the new spot and build our first
single-unit store.

It goes great, too. The very first day that store opens
for business, we sell every piece of chicken we have. The
same thing happens the second day. We sell so much
we have to go to the HEB grocery store and buy more
chicken because we can't keep up. I think it takes only
about three or four months and we've gotten all our
money back on the investment. We were the first fast-
food place in Laredo, and that store is still there.

⁓⁄⁄\⁓

A Shot Changes Everything

You probably remember exactly what you were doing when
you found out about the September 11 attacks, or, if you are old
enough, when John Lennon died, President John F. Kennedy was
shot, or Neil Armstrong and Buzz Aldrin landed on the moon.
Those moments are imprinted on our memories, the way a brand
is seared into the hide of a steer.

David and I were sitting in the workroom one afternoon, fuzzy
gray clouds hanging like dryer lint in the sky, and David was

telling me about the days in the mid- to late 1960s when Church's was rapidly expanding across South Texas. He spent a lot of time on the road, driving from one location to the next, helping to get fryers sizzling and cash registers ringing.

The expansion took place against a backdrop of racial unrest in America, and many of the restaurants were popping up along the fringes of black neighborhoods, where real estate cost less. Martin Luther King Jr. had won the Nobel Peace Prize in 1964 for his work to end racial inequality. The following year, he led marchers across the Edmund Pettus Bridge in Selma. He fought for desegregation, the right to vote, and equal treatment for workers of all races. Then, in late March 1968, King traveled to Memphis to support black sanitation workers who were on strike, demanding fair wages and treatment equal to that of their white counterparts. A few days later, on April 4, 1968, James Earl Ray shot King dead on the second floor of the Lorraine Motel.

⁓⋅⁄⋅⁓

In the spring of 1968, I spent a few weeks in Southeast Texas, opening a new store in Beaumont and another one in Port Arthur. Both stores were scheduled to open the same day. I always tried to attend the openings. Each one was a big deal to us. We put the Beaumont store in an underserved, predominantly black part of the city where it had virtually no competition. I'd hired the manager three months earlier and sent him to our training school in San Antonio. The crew didn't have much experience, though, and they needed some extra hands, so I stuck there through the noon rush on opening day. Everyone wanted that two-pieces-for-forty-nine-cents special, and we drew big crowds. We chalked up the opening as a big success.

Then I sped off to Port Arthur, arriving after the noon rush to an empty parking lot. All our stores back then were walkup. Customers would park outside and walk up to the window to order. We didn't have indoor seating or drive-throughs. The sight of that empty parking lot felt like someone had kicked me in the gut. Each opening played into our expansion plans, and if one store failed, we had to reassess. I wanted to call Bill with two success stories. This didn't look like one. I flung my car door open, ran to the serving window, and asked the manager what had happened.

"Mr. Bamberger, it was bad," he said, shaking his head. My stomach dropped. "They came and they came. They never stopped coming. We worked as fast as we could, until all of the fried chicken and fries were gone," he said. It's all about how you see it.

Those were halcyon days for me, but that feeling vanished back in my hotel room later that night, when I heard the news. Martin Luther King Jr. had been killed.

~/\\~

The Company Expands

Sales grew steadily. The company handed out raises. Incentives paid off. A manager in Atlanta became the first person to make it to Step 13 and buy his own Church's store without borrowing money. Five years after David joined the company, Church's started building stores with indoor seating. Ten years later, it introduced drive-through lanes so customers did not have to get out of their cars to pick up their chicken dinners. In Texas, Church's stores began popping up everywhere. The company began making what David described as "respectable money."

"When we started expanding, we discovered that we could open more stores and get a faster response by taking one major risk," he said. "We started positioning our stores in middle-income neighborhoods that closely bordered lower-income neighborhoods. There you could buy land for a fraction of the cost."

Those stores saw success. "Black people would come over to the white neighborhood to buy chicken. But if you put a store in a predominantly black neighborhood, white people wouldn't come over and buy there," he said. That success repeated around the country. The company claimed a high percentage of diversity among its employees, David said. In the 1970s, a black man, a Hispanic man, and a Korean man served on the company's board of directors. In the 1980s, a woman also served on the board. "Racism is rampant in America, but through our chicken company I wanted to make a statement about change," David said.

As Church's grew, David earned a reputation for his marketing skills. He developed a way of talking to people, no matter their position, that kept them entertained. They remembered Church's and David's homespun ways. They also remembered his creative marketing style. One of his marketing ploys involved honeycombed rock that David collected from his ranch near Bulverde, the same land that later became Guadalupe River State Park. He delivered a load of the pockmarked rock to Atlanta, where it was arranged in a display in front of one of his chicken stores that was to open the following day and advertised it as Texas moon rock. All this unfolded around the time that Neil Armstrong and Buzz Aldrin first walked on the moon, so it created a frenzy.

Overnight, the rock disappeared, stolen from its place of prominence next to the store. But that rock caused David a bigger problem—the attorney general in Georgia threatened to sue him for misleading advertising. The lawsuit did not stick because David advertised the attraction as "Texas moon rock" instead of simply moon rock.

The company did well. David never did get his two thousand dollars in loans back from Bill, but that did not really matter. In May 1969, with a fleet of about 110 stores, Church's made a public offering. Bill served as president and chief executive officer and chairman of the board; David became executive vice president and a board member. "The night before the offering, the original one-dollar shares were split into four shares. The first day out, each share sold for seventeen-fifty. The second day it was thirty dollars," David said. "I made sure every one of my store managers could have one hundred shares at twenty-five cents each."

Four days after Church's went public, David bought a ranch in the Texas Hill Country, just southwest of Johnson City. He named it Selah.

Amish Buggy

David sat at the desk in his workroom tucked beneath the garage at the ranch house at Selah. Through the wall of windows in front of him, he could see out over the ranch. Oak trees and native grasses spilled away before him, down hillsides and up ridges of green and gold and gray. He rifled through stacks of papers, sifted through letters he had collected over the decades, pointed out framed photos and documents hanging on the wall, then launched into another story.

⸻

In the early 1970s, I was building a fried-chicken store in Akron, Ohio. I went down to the Amish area of Ohio while I was up there, because I wanted to buy a buggy to put on the ranch. I found a shop that made them, and the guy who ran it came out to say hello. He was wearing overalls. I told him I came to see if he could build a buggy for me.

"Vell, that's what we do here," he said with a strong accent.

He pulled out his clipboard and asked me what I wanted on it. I didn't know you could get options on a buggy, but you could. It's like buying a car. I told him I wanted a front and back seat, but I didn't want curtains, because I wanted the passengers to be able to see out. He was eager to tell me about the other options that were available. He said, "Vell, we have hydraulic brakes, taillights, or a dashboard." I told him I'd just take it loaded.

He pulled out a postcard and had me fill it out with my name and address. "When the buggy is ready, I'll put this card in the mail to you," he told me. I asked him how long that might take. He told me maybe two months. Two months passed. Then three months, four months, and finally nine months. I went back to Akron to open the chicken store and decided to drive down to the buggy maker's shop to find out what was taking so long with my buggy. The same man came out, wearing what looked like the same pair of overalls. I looked at him, and he looked at me. I put my finger up to my cheek and asked him, "Do you remember this face? It's been nine months, and I haven't heard from you."

He looked at me long and hard. After a while he recognized me, I'm sure. But he wasn't all that worried about the delay in getting me my buggy. I soon found out why. It seems that my buggy was late because there had been too many weddings. In an Amish community, a young man can't get a buggy until he gets married. And when an Amish man gets married, his order gets priority over regular people like me at the buggy builder's shop. That meant a long wait to get that buggy to bring to the ranch.

Finally, though, it was ready. I waited until one of our delivery trucks was making a delivery to Akron, and since it was empty for the drive back, they loaded in my buggy for the trip to San Antonio. It sat in the parking lot at Church's headquarters for a couple of months. There was no explanation, but word spread like a prairie fire that Bamberger was doing something crazy again. Next thing I knew, someone put a Church's Chicken license plate on the back, and many times I saw one or two secretaries sitting in the buggy, getting their picture taken.

Eventually the buggy made its way to Selah, where we used it to carry Colleen Gardner, who later became the executive director of Bamberger Ranch Preserve, to her wedding ceremony on the porch of Hes' Country Store. That in itself was a beautiful and unusual day.

❋

Church's on the Rise

As time went on, the little chain of fried-chicken stores grew into a successful New York Stock Exchange company. At its peak, more than fourteen hundred Church's stores served fried chicken all around the world, from Puerto Rico to Australia. (Today, the international arm of the business is called Texas Chicken, and it has locations all over the globe, including Thailand, Iraq, and Egypt.) More than once, David found himself speaking to industry analysts, trying to explain the company's success. He hammed it up, employing his charm and folksy manner to woo the suit-and-tie set.

"I said many times, on Wall Street and in print, those Yale and Harvard guys knew how to work numbers, but they couldn't understand how we could build a four hundred–square-foot building, not bigger than this room we're in, into what it became. I always told them, 'Until somebody figures out how to sell chicken from a phone booth, this concept is still good.' And that turned out to be true."

The way David described it, business school graduates wearing three-piece suits made up most of those audiences. They touted their market savvy by crunching numbers but

David stands with the staff of one his fried-chicken stores in this undated photo. Courtesy David Bamberger.

demonstrated limited street smarts. One time, one of them stood up and waved a thick report. "Mr. Bamberger," he said, "I'm holding right here Kentucky Fried Chicken's marketing plan for this year. It calls for them to spend forty-three million dollars on television advertising in their markets in 1972. How does your little company plan to compete with this? What's your marketing plan, and how much will you spend?"

Bill and one of the Church's board members were attending the meeting with David. Someone kicked his leg under the table. They were worried. "Well, sir, thank you for your question," David said he told the audience. "I'm going to answer you, but I doubt you'll understand it." That was quite a putdown, David told me, but he took the risk, and continued. "Here it is in two sentences: Everyone who walks up to our window will get more for their money than a box of chicken, and everyone who walks through our back door to work will get more out of their job than a paycheck. We'll spend just one hundred thousand dollars on prizes and recognition for our employees."

The audience met that with silence. The young guy in a suit with the thick sheaf of papers stood up again. "You're right about one thing," he told the room full of people. "I don't understand it."

David decided to clear things up a little bit. "How can a customer get more for his money than a box of chicken?" he asked. "It's all about the people who work in that store. Customers walk up to a neat, smiling young man or woman, see spotless windows, no flies, and an uncluttered, tidy sidewalk. They order a forty-nine-cent box, and in twenty-seven seconds, someone hands them fresh, hot chicken. What a pleasant experience. One to come back to."

As for the employees? "We're doing everything we can to teach them basic business principles. We're recognizing their growth; we're encouraging them to save money; we're offering them unbounded opportunities to be an entrepreneur," David said. "These things aren't just incentives; they're making big people out of little people." David liked to repeat that mantra, which may sound dated today but reflected his belief that part of the company's success went back to hiring people who had come from less privileged backgrounds and had fewer career opportunities.

David had car license plates that read "49 to go," not only for the price of a two-piece dinner but also for the number of states where he wanted to build new stores. At that time, Church's had fried-chicken stores only in Texas. "I'll admit, for a while that was pretty heady stuff," David said, grinning.

But the luster of long hours spent at work, private planes, and big business deals started to fade. At about the same time, Bill, his partner, was getting heavily involved in Scientology, something that did not sit well with David. Bill got interested in other things that David did not understand—or want to understand—as Bill began traveling the state to learn about mind control. Finally, in 1973, David washed his hands of the fast-food chicken business. "I resigned my position as executive vice president and from the board of directors." Not long after his departure, Bill walked out, too. He skipped the annual board meeting and resigned via telegram. "You talk about havoc. The place was in an uproar," David told me.

For the next ten years, until 1983, David left the business of fried chicken to others. In 1976 he and several partners opened a restaurant in San Antonio called Mama's that featured a "bean burger," a meat patty topped with refried beans, crushed Fritos, guacamole, and picante sauce. (Mama's is still in business.) And he immersed himself in his Hill Country ranch, Selah.

For the first eight years of that period, Church's chugged along fairly well, but then it plateaued. Then someone knocked on David's door and said, "You need to come back to work." David returned as a member of Church's board of directors in 1983. At the time, David had more shares in the company than Bill Church did, but not more than the entire Church family as a whole. Within sixty days, the board named him chairman of the board and chief executive officer. He did not plan to stay long, just long enough to put a new management team in place. David later said he should never have gone back to Church's. But he did, and those first two years after his return rank as two of the company's top three performing years. Still, things had changed.

"A lot of new faces came in. When I left the company, everybody knew David Bamberger," he said. "It was different when I came back." New board members included people from all over the country. "Most of them weren't my kind of people," he said. "They thought we all had to have MBAs, and they couldn't see how you could run the company with what I called the 'unders'—under-educated, underprivileged, underserved people who had never had the opportunities we were making available to them." The marketplace had changed, too. Television held more influence, and technology was changing. It felt a little foreign to David.

David spent as much time as he could away from the office, working at what had by then become his true passion, Selah. When a reporter from *Barron's* phoned and asked him about the business, David did not hold back about his love of the land—and his waning interest in the fried-chicken business. He invited the reporter out to Selah. He told the reporter that Selah, to him, was like Walden Pond was to Thoreau. The resulting article quoted David as saying, "I'd rather be up here riding this tractor than sitting behind a desk in an office."

That message did not sit well with the company's stockholders and directors, and that, David believed, was what took him down. He was forced out as CEO, although he kept his position as chairman of the board and remained the company's single largest shareholder. That lasted only a few more months. When Popeye's bought out Church's in the late 1980s, David was gone "thirty seconds" after the buyout.

Popeye's Fried Chicken, the new parent company, began shuttering smaller, less productive Church's stores. Behind the scenes, David quietly began buying a few of those closed stores back, with plans of starting another fried-chicken company called Tu-Goes. He planned to go back to the basics. The Tu-Goes stores would have no indoor seating and no public restrooms. He bought three buildings but ended up selling them a year and a half later.

David's batter-coated finger seemed to have lost a little of its touch. Or, perhaps more precisely, he had lost interest in the fast-food business. David had plenty of money, but in his heart all he really wanted to do was plant trees and nurture the land. David went home to Selah and dove back into the country life.

Chicken Dinner with David

When you are friends with a man who began as a door-to-door vacuum cleaner salesman, then started a fast-food empire in the 1950s, you cannot resist an opportunity to share a box of fried chicken with him. I had never tasted Church's fried chicken that I could remember. Do not tell David, but I always liked Popeye's, probably because my husband grew up in Louisiana, where the company originated. So during a trip I took with David and Joanna to San Antonio in December 2017, we remedied that. After visiting the Christmas tree stand where David had volunteered for forty-four years, we needed a late lunch. I wanted some Church's. Joanna and David led the way, but when we pulled up to where the Church's that David wanted to visit should have been, we found a shuttered chicken shop. The restaurant had closed, and only an abandoned building and a Church's sign on a tall pole remained. Not a drumstick or jalapeño pepper in sight.

Miraculously, though (or perhaps by design), we wound up directly across the street from Mama's, the restaurant David and his partners had started in 1976, when he was on his ten-year sabbatical (as he called it) from Church's. We were drop-dead hungry, so we decided to go there for lunch first, then drive to a different Church's location a mile or two away for a box of fried chicken, just so I could taste it.

David wanted me to try the fried mushrooms at Mama's, and he was craving a bean burger—the delicacy straight off the Mama's menu that he and Joanna had previously prepared for me and Chris at the ranch. It was good. I ate a mountain of fried mushrooms, dipped in gravy, and half a bean burger. Then we loaded back into our car and drove down the road to another Church's location. All in the name of research, mind you.

We bellied up to the counter, and I started taking some pictures of David. People noticed, and I explained that the man at the counter was one of the people who got this very business going back in the 1950s. The customer in line behind me, impressed, pulled out his cell phone and began videotaping David, who ordered what he always does—a "wing breast," which is a wing

Pam and David sample fried chicken from a Church's restaurant in San Antonio, December 2017. Photo by Chris LeBlanc.

and a breast in one big piece of fried chicken. "That's the best buy. You can't get this piece of chicken at Kentucky Fried Chicken," he said, explaining in a nutshell the old Church's motto: "Big pieces. Little prices." He is immensely proud of that.

David ordered a jalapeño, too, and noted that one fiery little pepper, a staple on tables across Texas, contains more vitamin C than an orange. Church's had put peppers on the menu early on, and they were wildly popular in Texas (of course). But outside the state, most people had yet to acquire a taste for them. He went on to tell me a story about his once traveling to a Church's location in Dayton, Ohio, where he noticed that instead of the three- or four-gallon-sized containers of peppers that a typical Church's store in Texas would fly through in a week, it used only one container. He theorized that was just because Ohio residents had not been exposed to jalapeños and had no idea what they were.

All those years ago, he set to work to correct that. The Dayton

David orders chicken at a Church's restaurant in San Antonio, December 2017. The servers were surprised to hear they were ringing up an order for one of the company's cofounders. Photo by Pam LeBlanc.

store did not have indoor seating, and most of the clientele were blue-collar workers who came by at lunchtime, ordered from the window, and took their food back to their cars or trucks, where they sat behind the wheel to eat.

David determined he would introduce them to the glory of the jalapeño. In a somewhat sexist move, he arranged for a team of female employees, wearing hot pants and armed with plates of jalapeño slices with toothpicks piercing their green skins, to hand out samples to men eating chicken in their cars and on their tailgates. When those customers asked the employees what they were eating, they were told, "It's a Texas banana." The ploy worked. "I got the jalapeño pepper sales up there in Dayton almost as high as they were in Texas," David chuckled.

Back at the San Antonio location in 2017, I ordered a drumstick, and we got some biscuits. It came right up, hot and crispy, delivered by a smiling employee behind the counter, and we took it over to a proper table, where we sampled the food and I took some more pictures.

It tasted good to me, but David sensed something missing. When we stepped outside, he said, "The store was neat, and it was clean. The help was courteous—but that chicken. The grease was fresh, everything was good, but its flavor was not our flavor. That chicken's supposed to be marinated for twenty-four hours before it's cut up. That way it takes in the flavors." The chicken we bought that day, he claimed, was not properly marinated.

I did a little research afterward. Back when the company first started, Church's served just five things—chicken, fries, biscuits, jalapeños, and individual pies. Today, the menu has expanded. Besides original and spicy-flavor chicken, chicken sandwiches, boneless wings, and chicken strips, the restaurants sell chicken-fried steak, crispy or hand-breaded fish, mac and cheese, green beans, and more. The menu varies a bit by location. David rolled his eyes when I told him that. Too many things on the menu. Better to stick to the basics, he said.

I also learned that in 2017, Church's operated 1,650 locations in twenty-nine states and around the world. David couldn't believe it when I told him that Church's now had 64 stores in Indonesia, 42 in Malaysia, 30 in Saudi Arabia, and 15 in Guyana, and he definitely did not believe that 111 stores were selling Church's chicken in Puerto Rico. In 2017, Church's restaurants were located in Honduras, Bulgaria, New Zealand, Belarus, Thailand, Vietnam,

David took Pam to a Church's restaurant in San Antonio but said the chicken tasted like it had not been properly marinated. Photo by Pam LeBlanc.

Canada, the United Arab Emirates, Trinidad and Tobago, Pakistan, and elsewhere. That is a long way from home for a little fried-chicken restaurant that started in San Antonio.

Pants on Fire!

Even at ninety-two, David loves to tell jokes that might make your grandmother raise an eyebrow. When he told this one, I could easily picture him more than fifty years ago, not quite forty, getting a chuckle from something that happened during a business trip to Australia. Those early days were fun, David had explained to me. Things were happening, and clearly he loved the high-roller lifestyle and the attention he got for running such a successful business, at least for a time.

When I met him in the early 2000s, his energy seemed boundless, so it was easy to imagine him driving and flying and walking all over the globe, figuring out where to put chicken restaurants,

David enjoys a piece of fried chicken at a San Antonio location of Church's, since closed, December 2017. Photo by Pam LeBlanc.

how to get non-Texans to eat jalapeños, and what kinds of people to hire to make the stores successful. He did not want to sit behind a desk, crunching numbers or answering phone calls. He wanted to be part of the fried-chicken action, no matter where it took him. This is probably my favorite story that David told about his days wheeling and dealing in the fried-chicken business.

~٠٧٠~

Church's fried-chicken stores started popping up everywhere, and we expanded as far away as Australia. Sometime around 1971, we sent a man to Sydney, and he opened three stores that started doing pretty well. Based on that success, he decided he wanted to open some new locations in Perth. He scouted the city and snapped up six or seven tracts of land, all in prime locations. Then he hit some trouble trying to get building permits to put in the chicken stores. He asked me for help.

I decided to fly over and meet him, to help him get those permits. When we got to Perth, we checked into a brand-new high-rise hotel. We hauled our luggage up to our rooms on the fifteenth floor, about halfway up the building. Once we got settled in, we piled into a car and went for a ride to check out the tracts of land where he wanted the stores to go.

They all looked good, so we drove to city hall to talk about permits. That's where I smelled a rat. It turned out that one of the city council members owned a franchise for Kentucky Fried Chicken. Maybe that was why we couldn't get the building permits for our expansion. I called the local newspaper and told a reporter that politics had apparently interfered with business, and it wasn't right. Word got out, and a local TV station called me. The station wanted to send a crew over to interview us at the high-rise hotel. That was fine by me. But first, our suits needed cleaning.

We called down to the lobby and arranged to have someone come up and get our clothes and get them cleaned and pressed. We'd sit around in our undershorts while we waited for them to bring our clothes back. Someone came up and got our suits, and we started to wait. Minutes kept ticking away, and pretty soon it was almost time for the interview. Our suits still hadn't been returned.

The camera crew knocked on the door, cameras and tripods in hand. We let them in, wearing nothing but boxer shorts and white button-down shirts. We explained the situation. After a quick conference, the camera crew agreed that they'd film us from the waist up. Nobody would know that we weren't wearing clean pants.

We took the phones off the hook to make sure an incoming call wouldn't interrupt the filming. The camera crew leaned some equipment against the wall. We started the interview. A few minutes into it, the guy working the audio equipment started waving his arms. He flapped around, hopping up and down like a madman, trying to signal something to us. He must have been getting a message that we couldn't hear.

Then, wham! A big axe sliced through the door and in burst a bunch of firefighters wearing helmets. The heat from the cameras had set off the fire alarm. When hotel workers tried to check it out, they couldn't reach us because we'd taken the phones off the hook. An emergency team raced up to the fifteenth floor. We shot up off our seats—a bunch of guys wearing boxer shorts and neckties, and a crew with cameras pointed at them, filming the action. We had just one response, and we repeated it more than once. "This is not what you think. This is not what you think."

—⁓⁕⁓—

Giving Back with LOVE Lines

Throughout his life, David looked for people who needed a little help and gave it to them, whether it meant inviting underprivileged children to the annual spring picnic at Selah, standing up for someone who had been treated unfairly, or starting a charity at Church's that would do good in the community. In this story, he explained how a woman he saw perform at a club gathering inspired him to create a service arm at the fried-chicken company.

⸺ ⸳ ⸺

After I went back to work at Church's in 1983, I saw a woman perform at my Optimist Club meeting in San Antonio. She was deaf, and she danced and lip-synched along to the Kenny Rogers's song "The Gambler." It was beautiful watching her move her hands and express the meaning of the song. Afterward, she did a presentation, explaining a little more about her life. At home, she said, she had a system set up so that whenever her phone rang, the lamp in her room blinked. She couldn't hear but had a text telephone system set up so she could read what callers were saying to her.

It got me to thinking. About the time I met her, I was looking for a way for Church's to give back. McDonald's already had the Ronald McDonald House, and I thought Church's should pick a problem and make a difference too. I got in touch with the woman, and we came up with the idea for Lending Our Voices and Ears, or the LOVE Line.

We set up four text telephones in cubicles at Church's headquarters and went to work helping hearing-impaired people set medical and other appointments. With our help, a deaf person could pick up his or her phone, contact our LOVE line via a special telecommunications device, and a volunteer would then call the doctor's office to set up an appointment or make any other call that person needed. We staffed our lines with volunteers from 7:00 a.m. until 9:00 p.m. every weekday. We offered the program for free, and it didn't cost us much. We helped thousands of deaf people set appointments. That program lasted about five years before the State of Texas took it over.

~⁄₁⁀~

Sam Walton

David loved to tell stories about the people he met during his business career, both the ordinary people he encountered while selling vacuum cleaners and fried chicken and the big names. The way he described it, he treated those big names the same way he treated everyone else. And if he did not know them, he just introduced himself: for example, Sam Walton, the founder of Walmart and Sam's Club, who at one point during his life was considered the richest man in America.

Walton was a decade older than David, but the two had more than a few things in common. Walton was the son of an Oklahoma farming family. He grew up during the Great Depression, and like David, he did odd jobs to earn a little money for the family during tough times. He milked the family cow and sold the milk to neighbors, delivered the local newspaper, and sold magazine subscriptions before heading off to college as an ROTC (Reserve Officer Training Corps) cadet. While David started in the door-to-door vacuum business, Walton started by working as a manager of a variety store, then got a loan from a family member to buy his own small store. When he lost the lease on that one, he opened a store at a new location. Similar to the way David and Bill grew four tiny chicken shops into more than a thousand, Walton grew that one variety store into multiple stores, trying things that had never been done and enjoying remarkable successes along the way.

It seemed natural that the two entrepreneurs should eventually meet. David made sure it happened. The story illustrated another point. No matter the changes in technology, David always believed in the power of a handwritten note.

~⁄₁⁀~

In 1983, after a ten-year absence, or as I called it, sabbatical, I returned to Church's as chief executive officer and board chairman. Not long after my return, one of our board members, Jim Sperry, came to me. He'd been importing ceiling fans and noticed that the fans, which Walmart carried in their stores, sold better in smaller towns than big cities. He thought that if we got our chicken stores on Walmart pads, they would be very successful. Sperry had talked to the Church's real estate people, suggesting that they team up with Walmart, but those talks never went anywhere.

Thumbing through the pages of *Time* magazine on a flight to New York City for a meeting not long afterward, I noticed a picture of Sam Walton, Walmart's founder. Instead of the typical stuffy suit and tie, he was wearing a grass skirt in the photo—and he was dancing the hula on a little grass rug at the entrance to the New York Stock Exchange.

The story explained that the management team had summoned Walton to a meeting to tell him their data showed that they would earn 16 percent on sales in the coming year. That was an unbelievable amount, and Walton vowed that if they made those numbers, he'd do a hula dance on Wall Street. This was a guy I could relate to.

When I got back to the office that next Monday, I asked my secretary to bring me letterhead and a copy of our recent annual report. She brought them to me and sat down, waiting for me to dictate a letter. But I wanted to write this letter my way. In a handwritten note, I told Mr. Walton that I could put one hundred small fried-chicken stores on Walmart pads that very year. "If they don't make us both money, I'll pick them up and take them away," I wrote.

I paper-clipped that note to a copy of our annual report, which featured a photo of a huge crane lifting one of our all-in-one stores onto an empty lot on its front page. Then I called in Tom, our company pilot. I asked him if he'd ever flown the Learjet without a passenger. He had not. Then I asked him if he'd ever seen the TV program *Mission Impossible*. He had indeed.

"Tom, you're about to become a diplomatic courier," I announced. "Give me your arm." Tom held out the appointed limb, and I wrapped the envelope containing my note and the report around his arm, securing it with duct tape. "Now, you point that plane toward Bentonville, Arkansas, national headquarters of Walmart, and don't come back until Mr. Sam Walton gets this message," I told him. Tom asked politely if I was nuts. And maybe I was. I asked him to go anyway and to keep me posted.

At about 1:30 p.m., the phone rang. Tom had arrived at his destination, but he had a problem. He told me that Mr. Walton was traveling and not expected back until Friday. "Well, get a cot or a bunk somewhere and wait him out," I told him.

The next call came in at about 3:00 p.m. "Mr. Bamberger, we've got another problem up here," Tom said. I heard laughter in the background. Judd, the young (and handsome) copilot, had brought in ice cream for the office staff. Now Mr. Walton's assistant wanted to talk to me.

"Fine, put her on," I said.

The assistant wanted to know if I would call my boys home. I asked her if they'd become a nuisance. "Oh, no," she said. "They're perfect gentlemen. But they're distracting the staff."

I asked her if we could make a deal. I explained that the envelope Tom needed to deliver to Mr. Walton contained a two-sentence, handwritten note from me to him, one chairman to another. "Mr. Walton can read it in ten seconds," I said. "If you'll promise me that it will be the first thing he reads when he returns, I'll tell those young men to clear your office." She agreed. My boys came back to Texas.

Three days later, on Thursday morning, my secretary

appeared in my doorway, excitedly whispering that Mr. Sam Walton was on the line. I picked it up. The ready-made store idea intrigued the Walmart founder. He wanted to know details. I explained that we would make the buildings and deliver them directly to the sites. "We can get a store up and running in four or five days," I said.

He was interested. Then he told me that he owed me one. I asked him to explain. He told me his daughter had attended college at Trinity University in San Antonio. "We had her on a pretty tight budget, and every time we visited, she took us to Church's for that two-piece, forty-nine-cent box. She told us, 'I have to come here a lot.'"

Walton and I put our real estate people together and selected a few locations. Within a few months, and without all the negotiations and bureaucracy you'd need today, we put three new stores on Walmart pads. One of them was in booming Waxahachie, Texas, where construction was under way to build the Supercollider, a particle accelerator with a circumference of fifty-four miles. (Congress killed that project in 1993, leaving behind a huge, empty tunnel.) That Church's went on to deliver the highest return on investment of any Church's in the country.

‑⁊⫯⵩‑

4

David Turns His Focus to the Land

Although David got his start peddling vacuum cleaners and made his fortune selling fried chicken, the work he was most proud of, the work he hoped would stick with people who hear about it, has to do with land restoration and conservation. He had some fun making money, no doubt, but that money became a means to do what he felt was his most important life work. He wanted to nurture his land and show other people how they could do the same thing.

"It was my whole life's plan. I dreamed about all this years ago—not having money but getting the ranch and doing what I've done with it. Only through the hard work of building Church's, then selling it, could this have happened."

The German Storyteller

David loved to talk about Willie Stahl, the bent-over German who sold David his first ranch in 1959. Willie had thick fingers and a ruddy face and used a team of mules to plow the fields and plant cotton on his land. David took on the man's thick accent when he told his stories. "He had a hard life but was one of the most wonderful human beings I've ever met," David told me one morning while we were holed up in his workroom.

When David first bought Willie's property, he would bring his family and friends out to enjoy the 250-acre place along Cibolo Creek, right on the border between Bexar and Comal counties north of San Antonio. He called the ranch the Cinco B, for the five Bambergers—Donna and J. David and their three kids, Doug, Deena, and David. Visitors would poke around on the property, which included a grassy, fifty-acre field and an old camp, where they would dig up the occasional projectile point left there by Native Americans. David said he learned a lot from owning Willie's old place, and it motivated him to eventually get a bigger ranch. Ten years after he bought Willie's ranch, he bought Selah.

~\|/~

We all loved Willie Stahl. He was stooped from a lifetime of work, and his wife's name was Agnes. When I bought his place, I didn't have much money, and I had to borrow some from the bank. Another man had looked at the land, too. He'd offered Willie a lot more money than I could afford at the time. He was a distributor for Texaco Oil.

Willie didn't sell to him, and here's why. That man walked out behind Willie's old house and looked at the field where Willie once bent himself over planting cotton. He asked Willie the size of the field, because he wanted to put in a landing strip there. Willie didn't want an airstrip on the field he worked with his mules planting cotton all those years. That's why he sold the land to me.

When we went to the closing, I gave a key back to Willie. I wanted him to visit the ranch whenever he felt like it. And he did. He'd come out there every Sunday if he knew we were going to be there. Willie spent a lot of time at Specht's Store, a very small grocery, music, and beer joint not too far away where Willie Nelson had played when he was young. He'd tell people, "That Bamberger. He buy my place, and he give me the key back."

Willie Stahl told us all sorts of stories. He'd been out

there a long time and knew his neighbors. Back then, people in the country made whiskey. Smoke rose up off stills on every ranch. I asked Willie once if he ever had a still. He said in his accent, "No, but I make more damn money when all that was happening."

He told me he made his money by selling eggs. Then he explained. "I have a sign up that says 'Eggs—twenty-five cents a dozen.' Those Internal Revenue Service guys come out here, and they buy my eggs. I know they're looking for information, so I raise the price to thirty-five cents a dozen. They keep buying my eggs. I raise it to fifty cents a dozen." One day, those IRS men asked Willie if they could buy whiskey from anyone on the neighboring ranches. He tells them, "No, there's no whiskey selling out here."

They ask him again. "Mr. Stahl, you wouldn't tell us a story, would you?"

And here's what Willie does. He says, "Fellas, Willie Stahl never will tell a lie," and as he said it, he took a little hop to demonstrate, then finished his sentence—"in this place." That was just one Willie Stahl story.

My wife, Donna, and I had three kids. She was a Girl Scout leader. We'd take the Girl Scouts to the ranch because we could get there in about twenty minutes from our house in San Antonio. One day when Donna was bringing the Scouts out there, she asked Willie if any snakes lived on a fifty-acre field on the property. Willie said, "Oh, no. There's no snakes over there; they're all over there in Bexar County, on the other side of the creek." So she headed out with the girls, and they camped out in this old shackwhere some of the girls found a snakeskin.

Donna found Willie afterward and said to him, "You told me there were no snakes out here."

"I did?" he asked.

"Yes, you did," Donna told him. "You said all the snakes were over there in Bexar County. My Girl Scouts were over at the old Indian Camp, and they found a snakeskin."

Willie got a big chuckle out of that. "Oh, vell, they didn't find a snake then, did they?" he said.

⁓⁄⥿⁓

David also bought property on the Guadalupe River in the Hill Country. "I owned a beautiful part of the river," he said one day. "I could have held on to that land and sold it for millions of dollars. But I wanted to say something about the need to set these kinds of things aside." He decided to try to sell the land at a low price to the State of Texas to create a park.

His neighbors in nearby Spring Branch back then did not want a park, David said, because they worried it would bring in the hippies with all their trash. They protested against it. It took two years, but David ultimately did sell the state his 505-acre parcel. Today crowds flock to Guadalupe River State Park near Bulverde every summer to dip a toe in the cypress-lined river or grill hamburgers beneath a canopy of oak trees.

The Most Important Work

In the late 1960s, just before Church's went public, David began looking around Central Texas, searching the Hill Country for something nobody else wanted. He settled on an old cattle ranch nestled in a ring of hills just south of Johnson City. As he walked the property in 1969, trying to decide if this was the place to begin the biggest challenge of his life, the one that made vacuum cleaners and chicken shops fade into the background like sunbleached wallpaper behind a bright framed painting, he saw thousands of acres of promise.

Water hardly flowed. Wildlife was scarce. But David remembered the book his mother had given him to read, Louis Bromfield's *Pleasant Valley*. In that book, Bromfield wrote about returning to the Ohio farmland where he grew up. He found the old farm fields abandoned, victim to farmers who did not yet understand the science behind crop rotation. They had planted the same crops again and again, robbing the soil of needed nutrients. When

Bromfield returned, the old farmland lay fallow. Bromfield wanted to put into practice what he learned while living in France, where farmers better understood how to keep soils productive from one generation to the next.

He bought his grandparents' farm and two contiguous farms in northern Ohio and set about restoring the land, using the techniques of those European farmers. He rotated crops and spread organic fertilizer, and over time the land came back. He invited the public to see what he was doing, and his reputation grew. People came to know him as someone who injected life back into a place that others had neglected. When President Franklin Roosevelt offered Bromfield the position of secretary of agriculture, Bromfield turned it down.

David envisioned a Texas version of Bromfield's great Ohio experiment. He already had a name picked out for the ranch: Selah, a biblical term that means to pause or reflect. It would be his version of Thoreau's Walden Pond. He wanted to pump life back into the hot, sunbaked country of Central Texas, where scrub cedar and other woody species had spread. He wanted to reseed native grasses to stop the erosion that had taken away what little soil was there. He wanted to turn this land around and demonstrate to others what could be done with overgrazed, mistreated property.

And, slowly, he did. He began removing some of the invasive species, taking out much of the water-hungry Ashe junipers, commonly called cedar trees, but leaving them in canyons, where they naturally occurred and where the endangered golden-cheeked warblers could pull strips of bark from mature trunks to use for nest-building material. Cedars caught rainwater in their nubby, needlelike "leaves." Much of that moisture never made it into the soil, evaporating when the sun came out and a breeze ruffled the plant structure. In contrast, the long, fringy networks of the roots of native grasses held moisture in the ground, where the land—and animals, by extension—could benefit from it.

A more balanced, healthy ecosystem gradually returned to Selah. The deer grew fatter, and bird counts increased from 48 species when David got the ranch to 218 species in 2019. Springs began to flow. When that happened, David invited people to take notice. Early on, when people visited Selah, they knew two things about David: one, that he had started a chain of very successful fried-chicken restaurants; and two, that he had a lot more money than they did. The latter, they usually believed, meant they could never make the same impact or improvements on the land that he did.

David did not believe that. From his pulpit at Selah, he tried to show people that they could make a difference too, even if they did not have a lot of money or own a sprawling ranch in the Hill Country. "I want to tell them you can do everything I've done with your own property," he said. "Invariably they say, 'I don't see how you can believe that. I can't afford a bulldozer.' I ask them, 'How many acres do you have?' When I get a reply, I say, 'You don't need a bulldozer. You need chainsaws and wheelbarrows and axes and shovels—and a bunch of friends.'"

And then he offered suggestions. They could gather native grass seeds from highway right-of-way lands. They could plant that seed on their own smaller parcels of land, instead of planting water-hogging St. Augustine grass. They could reuse and repurpose things and conserve resources. They did not always need a bulldozer, just a wheelbarrow, picks, shovels, and rakes. "If you have the tolerance for the frustration and inconvenience used equipment can sometimes bring, you can buy it for thirty cents on the dollar," he said.

To be a conservationist, he believed, you love the natural world and do right by your neighbors, which does not take tons of money. It just takes commitment. "What I have inherited is all around you today," he said, raising his arms to indicate the land, the trees, the sky, the whole natural world. "It's the love and respect for Mother Nature that becomes so important to our lives."

Ranch Lessons

You learn a lot by running a ranch, as David could tell you. He was explaining this one day, pointing out some fences on the property on a warm summer day. Equipment is expensive, he said, and it pays to repurpose and reuse things. It also pays to hire people who understand that and can teach it to others.

"The fences here are made with repurposed cable, eye bolts, and telephone poles," he told me as we drove along, and he waved his arm out the truck window as fence line scrolls past. "New, a single eye bolt would cost five-fifty." But Leroy Petri, a valued Selah employee who has worked on the ranch for decades, bought a bunch of them, castoffs from old telephone poles, for just five cents a pound, David tells me. That's a huge savings.

"Same story with the cable that anchors the fences," David said. He pointed out some old telephone poles, also repurposed. It is like that all over the ranch and a lesson David likes to share with visitors. Do not buy new stuff. Give old stuff new life. With that he segued into a story about his son Doug, who learned a lot of lessons from Leroy as he struggled to get his own life back on track.

⁓⫶⁓

This ranch saved my son's life. Doug got into some trouble with drugs at a very young age, when he was a preteen. His mother handled it better than I did. We ended up in counseling with other parents whose kids were troubled. Doug had enough intelligence to know when he was getting himself in too deep, and when that happened, he would come back home and announce he was going to go out to the ranch. But he wouldn't stay very long, and the whole cycle would start all over again.

Donna and I were in counseling, learning how to handle Doug's problem. The next time he came home and said, "I'm going to the ranch," I said, "No, Doug. We need your help up there for longer than just a day or two. I'll make a contract with you. If you'll stay six months, I'll give you the ranch truck, the hunting cabin, and seventy-five dollars a week." Doug ended up staying three years. He learned a lot of things during that time. He learned how to run a backhoe, and he learned how to be an electrician, a carpenter, and a farmer. He also learned to appreciate the natural world.

One time, Leroy was driving a trailer carrying some calves down to the market in San Antonio. As they drove toward Blanco, Leroy saw some men working on power lines off on the side of the highway. He said to Doug, "Remember this spot." They went to San Antonio, unloaded the calves, got something to eat, and started driving back to the ranch. By this time it was after 5:00 p.m., and the guys who had been working on the side of the road were done with their work. Leroy remembered exactly where they had been working. He pulled the truck over at that spot and got out to look for tools the men might have left behind.

Sure enough, he and Doug picked up three tools that the crew had missed. Leroy's message was this: "Too many people, they've got a job, but they don't respect what they have. They're more interested in getting off the clock and going home." His lesson to Doug was important. "We work for your father, and he had to pay good money to buy good tools, and it's up to us to maintain them," he told him.

Leroy is an unbelievable human being. He could build an interstate highway. He's bought himself two paddle scrapers, one with air-conditioning and a stereo. He owns a bulldozer bigger than the one I have. He owns three articulating frontend loaders. He owns dump trucks and two motor graders. If you had to buy all of his equipment new today, it would cost you a couple million lars, and he doesn't owe a penny on it. He picks up aluminum cans and really knows how to recycle. I introduced him to a surplus lot in San Antonio, and I think he practically bought them out. He has saved me so many thousands of dollars over the years.

Doug eventually moved to Kerrville, where he went to work at a hardware store. In the meantime, I had formed a family corporation in the 1970s that we called

Entre Nous, which is French for "among ourselves." It
served as a vehicle to teach the children stewardship of
money and to provide financial support if they wanted
to go into business, but only if they proved themselves
first.

When a hardware store in Blanco came up for sale,
I drove to Kerrville and asked Doug, who had finally got
okay and earned a high school diploma from an alterna-
tive school, "How'd you like to manage a hardware store
in Blanco?" Our little corporation bought that store and
put him in as manager, with a contractual agreement that
he could earn ownership of it over a period of years, just
like my Step 13 program at Church's.

People who focus only on the money David made confound him.
He is fiercely proud of his roots, the lessons he learned growing
up in poverty, not even realizing then what it meant to be "poor."
"I look back on it now with pride, because there were so many
lessons I didn't know I was learning until I had Selah, and I paused
and I reflected on life and what's it all about," he told me. He wants
the next generation to learn those lessons too.

For years, a group of high school students came to Selah for
a weeklong camp. One year, a man knocked on the door of the
ranch house, two teenagers in tow. The man had come to Selah
for one of those camps back in the 1970s. Now he had his own
two children with him, and he wanted to show them something
about the work he had done at Selah when he was their age. "I've
been telling my kids about the dams we built for stopping erosion," he told David. "They're curious about them. I was wondering if you'd let me show them."

David understood that the father and his children wanted to
go alone, and he let them, as long as they promised to stop back
by on their way out. "About two and a half hours later he's back
at my doorstep," David told me. "He couldn't find those dams. So
I take him down to the spot. He knew where those dams were,
but he couldn't find them because they had worked so well since

he made them." David got down on his knees and parted the grass, exposing gullies filled with stones. In the three decades that had passed since that man had helped build those dams, rain had fallen, and water had carried seeds down into the pockets between the rocks. Grasses had grown. A living blanket now concealed the long-ago work.

"Heck of a story for those little children—and for anyone who wants to save soil," David said. That's what he wanted to pass on. The knowledge that given a little boost, protected from harm, nature will return to a healthy balance. He also knew that we need nature as much as it needs our help right now. It is the reason that David abided by what he called "The Declaration of Dependence." "I'm dependent on the natural world," he said, and I understood what he meant. I felt the same way. Talking to David reminded me that we all need nature, no matter to which generation we belong.

When people come to Selah to visit, David wants each one to experience what he describes as a "Selah moment," a moment of reflection, a memory that he or she will carry home long after driving away, passing under the sign above the white gate that says "Vaya con Dios." Visiting school groups pause at the end of their trips to think about what has meant the most during the time they have spent at Selah. After a few minutes of thoughtful silence, the students and their teachers pick up their pencils and write down a few thoughts. Sometimes they pen a handwritten note to Water, around which everything at Selah seems to revolve.

David chuckled when he thought about those messages, which have included, over the years, a little boy who wrote to ask if Water would come with him to the movies the next day. Or the letter from another student, which went something like this: "Dear Water, you're so, so beautiful. You're such a big part of me. I wish I could take you home with me, but I do want to confess and apologize for one thing—tinkling in you when I swam."

Those notes mean a lot, because they bring home the lessons that David learned as a boy, lessons he has passed to people like me and all who visit Selah. And to David that is a lot more important than fried chicken and vacuum cleaners.

Cedar: The Root of Many Problems

Just about everyone who comes to Selah visits Madrone Lake, where one of the ranch employees—or, if lucky, David himself—gives a short demonstration to show why native grasses are so important and why too many cedar trees can spoil a chunk of Hill Country land. This is how it works: A small Ashe juniper, commonly known as a cedar tree, is planted in a Plexiglas box. Native grasses are planted in an adjacent box. A system rigged up above the boxes acts as a rainmaker, and when someone flips a switch, "rain" sprinkles down on the trays below.

Within a few seconds, the water sprinkled onto the cedar tree drips off its nubby fingers, falls onto the ground, runs through the barren soil, and drips rapidly out the bottom of the box, taking eroded soil with it into the jar below. The tree does not support a fine enough network of roots, and grass cannot grow beneath the cedars because it does not get enough light.

But when it "rains" onto the tray planted with grass, the water stays in the soil much longer, where it feeds the grass and keeps the soil moist. The delicate, branched root system of the grass, which David says constitutes about ten times the volume underground as it does above, slows the flow of water and filters it along the way. Seven minutes later, a little clear—not muddy—water then slowly drips into the jars below. That demonstration shows vividly the value of grass, which David describes as "the greatest conservation tool of all." It is also cheap. On a small scale, planting native grass does not require a huge investment of money, yet it can make a huge difference.

Cedars still serve a vital purpose in the Hill Country, and David does not suggest that every last cedar tree be unceremoniously ripped from the ground. Cedars once grew here naturally, mainly in canyons. Those trees grew to maturity, and native (now endangered) golden-cheeked warblers pulled long strips of bark from the thick trunks of mature trees and used them to build nests. Grasses covered broader swaths of land back then and helped move more water into what biologists call a perched aquifer just 125 feet deep. "The key to getting water into the ground is slowing it down," says Steve Fulton, the towering ranch manager at Selah. "Cedar just doesn't slow it down, but grass does."

The Hill Country was once predominantly grassland, kept in that state by occasional wildfires and large migrating buffalo herds. More than 150 years of fire suppression and overgrazing by cattle caused a transformation, from grasses to the cedar forests that replaced them and that covered the land David purchased. But just a few years after he removed much of the cedar at Selah and planted twenty thousand dollars' worth of grass seed, the habitat rebounded and wildlife began to return. Here is how David told me the story.

~✦~

When I bought this ranch, only forty-eight species of birds lived out here, according to counts by the Audubon Society. The biggest deer weighed fifty-five pounds. There was nothing for the deer to eat. There was no water. How could a deer live without water? Hunters,

David hikes at Selah, April 2017. Photo by Pam LeBlanc.

who paid three thousand dollars for a hunting lease, wouldn't return after the first year.

When the Hill Country was first settled, it had tall grasses and water and looked good, but even the Germans misjudged how delicate it was. We put too much livestock on this fragile country. With fences, overgrazing, and the suppression of fires, one of the only plants that really survived here was the cedar tree.

Cedar's a native tree, an evergreen woody species whose root system goes as deep as the soil it grows in. Deer don't eat it, and cows don't eat it. The only part that the golden-cheeked warbler uses is the bark, which it uses to make a nest. At Selah, we cleared more than three thousand acres of cedar. We left it growing in some places. I didn't remove any of the old growth. I've got one cedar tree down there you and I can't even wrap our arms around. That's the kind that built the Texas Capitol. I have a grove that I kept as cover for animals trying to move across the ranch. And it grows naturally in canyons.

Once we started clearing the cedar and seeing grass cover on the land, we began getting the water. The habitat came back, and things changed. The animals returned. The birds came in. The number of bird species alone has increased to more than two hundred. Now we're harvesting deer that weigh 155 pounds, and we bring in up to eighty thousand dollars annually from hunters' leases. Back when I bought the property, it took forty-one acres to support a single cow. Now it takes just eighteen.

Landowners with a lot of cedar on their property should clear it in areas where the soil could produce something else, like native grass. There is nothing you can do that works as quickly and inexpensively as grass. Conservation is not only good for Mother Nature; it's good for your bank account.

Fall Comes to Selah

The second time I met David, he was sprinting down a trail at Selah, drawn toward a cluster of trees ablaze in fall color. "Another maple, another maple," he whooped and hollered, a shock of white hair flapping as he ran. He was eighty-five years old then and still moved so fast he left most of the people who had come to Selah for a fall color tour in his dust. "You just have to look at this. It's unbelievable!"

For a day or two each fall, David opens the gates at Selah, inviting the public to soak up the crimson, orange, and yellow canopy on his land. He told me often that "places like this shouldn't be locked up and kept only for rich people." That is why the ranch occasionally hosts public tours, brings in schoolchildren to experience ranch life, and offers educational programs. And that is why the land has been set aside as a preserve for future generations.

During the color tour that day in 2013, I got the distinct impression that even after eight decades on planet Earth, David still found it hard to believe that fall actually had come once again

David and Joanna lead a group of hikers on a fall color tour at the ranch, November 2013. Photo by Tino Mauricio.

and that those trees were dressing themselves in brightly colored jackets in the form of leaves. He and Joanna raced down the trail, practically vibrating with excitement each time they encountered a newly turned tree. "Look at that, David. They have come out!" Joanna said that day, trotting close behind. For them, every tree, crackling twig, and cool breeze demanded attention. At one point, they each grabbed a branch from a bigtooth maple and kissed the fiery, five-lobed leaves.

David caught the bigtooth maple bug in the early 1990s. At the time of the tour I have just described, he had already planted more than four hundred of the trees and had nine more ready to put in the ground. Some now stand forty feet tall. He has carefully tagged and numbered each one and recorded its planting date. They are the same type of tree that draws throngs of leaf peepers to Lost Maples State Natural Area on the Edwards Plateau near Vanderpool every fall. That population is the largest natural

David sits on what he calls "the butt bench" above Madrone Lake, pointing out the cypress trees he and the Tree Aggie, Jim Rhoades, "planted." Photo by Pam LeBlanc.

concentration of bigtooth maples in Texas, but David believes his is the largest introduced population. "People say I'm crazy, but I'm building a forest," he told me then, blue eyes flashing. "I planted every one myself."

The maples at Selah have proven hardy. About two thousand Spanish oaks on the ranch died during the devastating 2011 drought, but just one bigtooth maple was lost. The trees grow well if planted in the right place, and they are relatively drought and heat tolerant. The biggest challenge is keeping white-tailed deer from snacking on their foliage, which must taste like maple syrup to them.

Back during that tour, David, ever the consummate showman, apologized because the woods were not fully ablaze just yet. The trees' color typically peaks in early November. "I'm sorry it's not every tree, but that's Mother Nature," he told a couple who had stopped to admire a particularly vibrant specimen. "They were all supposed to be like this."

Still, the show drew ooohs and aaahs from those who came to look, and that's what David was after. "Don't go to Vermont to see the maples," he told the crowd. "Come to Selah." Better yet, the implied message went, turn your plot of land, your yard, no matter how small, into a sort of preserve. Plant native grasses, take out invasive species, and do what you can to bring wildlife back. Here is David's take on a quick way to plant trees.

— ∕∕ —

Jim Rhoades, the man I call my "Tree Aggie" because he's my tree expert and he graduated from Texas A&M University, showed up at the ranch one Saturday morning with two five-gallon pickle buckets full of black, rather smelly muck. He says, "Dave, how would you like to plant five thousand trees today?" to which I say, "Tree (that was my nickname for him), what have you been smoking?" Jim tells me he's been wading in the creek at Brackenridge Park in San Antonio. Bald cypress trees shroud the creek there on both sides. It's like being inside a tunnel. Well, seeds had been falling off these trees by the thousands. Eddied up by the stream, they'd clustered together, and Jim goes on to tell me that his two buckets are filled with muck he scraped from that creek. "There are thousands of seeds in this muck," he tells me.

That really intrigued me. Leroy had just finished building the dam at Madrone Lake, and the water was up. What did we have to lose? Jim and I headed off to the lake. I followed his example by reaching my hands into that bucket of muck, and together we threw handfuls

David hugs a towering tree at the ranch, April 2017. Photo by Pam LeBlanc.

of that stuff into the water. As the muck hit the water, it released the seeds, which floated to the surface while the rest of the stuff sank to the bottom. Over the next few days, the wind and water pushed those cypress seeds ashore, where nature went to work. They settled into the dirt on the banks of the lake, sprouted, and set down roots.

Eventually, one hundred little bald cypress trees grew up ringing the lake. That's when we really went to work. We dug most of them up and moved them all around the ranch. We left about two dozen trees at the lake, where you can see them today. Some of them are fifty feet tall.

~/|\~

Hanging Out with the Tree Aggie

"Trees, I love trees," David tells me one day as he pulls his beat-up old pickup truck onto the edge of a grassy field across from Hes' Country Store. He shows me a series of spindly trees sprouting around the field, each one encircled by a wire cage to protect it from hungry critters. "I'm planting my own forest," he tells me. So far, he has stuck forty-eight trees in the ground here—oaks and elms and maples and more. Before he is done, he plans to plant one of every type of tree that is native to Blanco County, right there in that field. The forest will stand as a kind a memorial to his mother, who loved trees and passed on that love to her son.

"People say, 'Dang it, Bamberger, you come up with some dumb stuff,'" David tells me. "But I want to build this so people can come out here and take a workshop. When they take that workshop, they'll get a pamphlet with an identification key that helps them learn how to identify different species. Then they can walk up to a tree they've never seen before, ask the questions from the key, and it'll lead them to the answer as to what kind of tree it is."

Trees rank right up there with people in David's world. He loves to plant them, check on them, and, when they are young, pour water on them when they need it. But only until they reach a certain age. Then they are on their own. Plenty of what he has learned about trees came from the man he calls his Tree Aggie.

_◦◦◦_

It's not often that such an unforgettable character comes into your life—especially one who for years has given you his time and talent nearly every weekend, teaching you valuable lessons about trees, lessons that you pass along hundreds, maybe thousands, of times to other interested landowners. This man was Jim Rhoades. Because of his degree in urban forestry from Texas A&M University, everyone referred to him as the "Tree Aggie" and, later on, just as "Tree."

Though there certainly isn't any rocket science to planting a tree, the first lesson I got from Jim Rhoades was a surprise—"Dig a square hole." The explanation was simple. Every plant you purchase comes in a round container. Depending on how long the plant has been in it, its roots will develop in a circular fashion. For rapid growth, you want those roots to branch out in all directions.

We've planted more than six thousand trees and shrubs on the ranch, and whenever we lose one, sometimes five years later, we dig it up to see if we can figure out what killed it. Surprisingly, some seemed to have strangled themselves. The roots continued growing in that circular pattern after they were planted. It's our policy not to continue watering after a plant's second year, and our "autopsy" sometimes showed that a tree or shrub didn't spread its roots far and wide enough to hold on to life when a hot, dry drought period came along. And those periods do come along.

Another way to encourage a tree to spread its roots is to place a large flat flagstone, which we have plenty of here at Selah, in the bottom of a hole where you plan to plant a tree. While I'm religious about the square hole, I don't always use this flat stone trick, and never do when planting a taproot tree like a pecan or a bur oak. Jim also said that most people plant their trees too deep, and I was guilty of that. He said that most trees settle down at least an inch within three months of planting. Planting them too deep and not allowing for that sinking puts the small trunk in jeopardy.

Back in the 1970s and '80s, Jim worked for the Austin Parks and Recreation Department as an urban forester, and he found himself under pressure from developers and some of the big retailers who wanted to cut down trees and also from the other side—the activists who fought hard over keeping trees. When big-box retailers or gas stations wanted to bulldoze out big, beautiful trees to make room for their buildings, one man stood in the way—Jim Rhoades, the only tree expert in the department at the time. Jim had to attend many late-night city council meetings. He proposed a compromise. For each big tree a company removed, it would have to replace it by planting many others. This policy helped move the city forward.

There's plenty more to learn from the Tree Aggie, but who would guess it would involve the naming of a highball? In the early 1980s, Donna and I lived in San Antonio but spent weekends at the ranch. Jim was single and lived in Austin in the smallest apartment I'd ever seen. It was maybe eight hundred square feet, spread onto two levels, with the living area a ten-inch step down from the kitchen.

Jim proudly invited Donna and me to dinner one night. He didn't have any culinary skills but knew of an entrepreneur who started a business named Highway Pizza. He picked up one of those pizzas and brought it home for us, but before we sat down to enjoy it, he offered us a drink. I asked if he had bourbon. We weren't party folks or big drinkers, but we did enjoy an occasional whiskey sour. "Jim," I asked, "do you have 7UP or

Sprite to mix with the bourbon? That would taste good."

In short order, Jim handed each of us an iced-tea glass of bourbon mixed with Sprite. This was a big glass. While we talked and watched Jim set the table and bring forth the Highway Pizza, we sipped on that extremely strong drink. It hit us before dinner was served. As we moved to the living area of Jim's bachelor apartment, Donna and I discovered we were both a bit tipsy. We missed the ten-inch step and fell to the floor. From that night on, we called a very strong bourbon over ice floating in Sprite a "Jim Rhoades."

Now this may be hard to believe, but we have ordered a Jim Rhoades in many restaurants. The classic case came in Alpine, Texas. We were there looking for an endangered plant, the Murray plum, when one evening we walked into a restaurant then called the Cinnabar at the Holland Hotel, a historic old downtown building. The waitress asked us if we'd like a drink, and I said, "Yes, we'll each have a Jim Rhoades." She dutifully wrote the order down, and we watched the bartender search through his book. Remember, Alpine is a small West Texas town. The waitress returned and very apologetically told us how sorry she was, but the bartender didn't know this drink.

We had had trouble finding a place to stay for the few nights we were in Alpine because Willie Nelson was coming in the next week to start filming a movie. The advance production people had taken all the motel space. "Well, young lady, you know everyone in Alpine is excited about Willie Nelson coming to town," I told her. "The Jim Rhoades is very popular with Willie and his crew, so let me give you the recipe." I described the drink, and she wrote it down like it was gospel—"two shots of good bourbon over ice, add four ounces of diet Sprite, and serve with twist of lime."

I don't believe Willie Nelson ever ordered a Jim

Rhoades, but maybe the restaurant presented him with one. What I do know is that the "recipe" was in fact written into the bartender's little book. Here's how I know: My oldest son, David K., and three other young men get together each year for a high school friends' reunion. One year David tells me they are going to West Texas, somewhere around Alpine. I ask him to visit the Cinnabar and order a Jim Rhoades. They do, and sure enough, the waitress proudly delivers four perfect Jim Rhoades to their table.

5

Selah

When you live in Texas, you get used to summers so hot that every patch of pavement feels like a sizzling griddle, and walking down a city street beneath a blazing sun sucks the life right out of you. That time of year, I plan my life around swimming opportunities. As it happens, one of the finest swimming holes I have ever dipped a toe in is located right there at Selah. I think I started salivating the first time David drove me down to Madrone Lake, which was where he put on his rainwater demonstration, showing ranch visitors how the roots of native grasses help hold moisture in the soil. It is a human-made lake the size of three or four football fields.

While David was pontificating about the importance of grasses that day in front of a small audience, I kept gazing over his shoulder at the lake, a glimmering oasis of green. Soil is important, I know, but at that particular moment, I really wanted to go for a swim. I needed to get in that water and float for a while, and I needed to squint up at the sun and admire the ring of cypress trees growing around the perimeter of the lake. Trees, I later learned, that David planted by heaving a mucky bucket full of dirt and seeds into the lake.

Gretch Sanders watches as Pam jumps off the swim platform at Madrone Lake. Photo by Chris LeBlanc.

I did not get to swim that first day at Selah (the lake is private, and you need permission to swim there), but months later I finally got to take a much-anticipated flying leap into Madrone Lake. It felt as good as I knew it would. The swim platform there is the stuff of dreams, anchored by a pair of chains wrapped around weights sunk to the bottom of the lake. The platform itself drifts about twenty feet from where a stone path leads to the water. Two metal ladders are attached to the platform, so it is easy to haul yourself up onto the wooden deck. In a light wind, it rotates slowly, like a dog on a leash, eager to run out ahead. Usually in the morning, big spiders have spun cobwebs across the handles of the ladder.

The more time I spent at Selah, the more I swam in that lake. It quickly became a habit, when I was staying at the guesthouse, to get up early, run to the lake, jump in for a swim, and run back. Along the way, I would soak up as much of the ranch atmosphere as I could. As I stumbled along, a few deer would bound across the field in front of me, flipping up their flag-like white tails. Occasionally I had to plunge through a small herd of cattle, steeling my nerves but knowing—according to Steven Fulton, the ranch manager, anyway—that they would ignore me. (They always did.) I might hear an owl hoot or find a turtle on the side of the road.

Once, on a chilly mid-November morning, I ran to the lake, dipped a toe in the brisk water, then gave in to it. I had not planned on swimming—it was November, after all—but this being Texas, I did anyway. I plunged in, among the mats of green and gray and flickering underwater rays of light. Another time, I spotted something hanging from a tree branch across the water. I swam over slowly, knowing what I would find before I even got there: a snakeskin as long as a person, caught on the branches, flapping like a banner. Always, there were turtles. And a forest of plants sprouted from the bottom of the lake, tickling my toes.

All those experiences, for me, were magic. They reminded me of the importance of nature, something that David tries to impress on everyone who comes to Selah. We need to protect the land. We need places like this, where birds and insects and skunks and snakes can live how they are supposed to live. We need places like this, where humans can scrape their shins on

Pam swims at Madrone Lake, summer 2017. Photo by Chris LeBlanc.

Pam leaps into Madrone Lake, one of her favorite spots on the planet. Photo by Chris LeBlanc.

rocks and let the wind tangle their hair and feel the bite of ants on their ankles. We need to go outside, feel the scorching sun, touch the muddy ground, wade into a creek, or climb up a hillside. We need to see the little things that live under rocks and fly through the sky and trot through the canyons. At places like Selah, we can do that.

Sometimes Cell Towers Bring Good News

As long as David has been restoring Selah and telling people about it, a steady stream of curious landowners, environmentalists, plant lovers, and nature seekers have called the ranch or driven to its gates, asking to see it. David's late wife, Margaret, whom he married after he and Donna divorced, came up with the idea of offering group tours as a way of both bringing in a few dollars and sharing information about conservation in a more efficient way. According to her plan, everyone would meet at the ranch on a Saturday morning. For a five-dollar donation to cover costs, staff employees would pull visitors around in a hay trailer for three hours and answer all their questions.

"I never thought that would work, but we gave it a try," David told me one day, as he climbed into his truck to head down to Hes' Country Store, where he planned to meet a tour group and tell a few stories. "We figured forty people could fit on the hay bales, and surely that would be a lot more room than we needed. But thirty minutes before the scheduled tour that first Saturday, cars and trucks started rolling in. I put a call out on the two-way radio for someone to bring over another trailer. That one filled up, too."

The tours still take place several times a year. And instead of sitting on hay bales, visitors now climb into the Bluebonnet, an open-air trailer outfitted with long bench seats and pulled behind one of the ranch trucks. "We've raised the cost a little bit, which has helped us break even on them," David says. "And someone else leads the tours these days, although I sometimes show up at Hes' Country Store to introduce myself." If you have met David, you know that an "introduction" at the store usually turns into an hour or two packed with stories, memories, maybe a little coffee or tea, and plenty of laughs.

—◦—

I'm not religious, but God just seems to take care of me and I don't know why. A man named Chap calls me on a beautiful Sunday morning. He lives in Houston but has just purchased two hundred acres near Stonewall. He's heard about Selah and wants some advice about how to make similar improvements at his new ranch. He had tried to register for one of our education workshops, but he travels so often for work that he can't make any of the dates work with his schedule.

"I know that this is an imposition, but could we come over to your ranch this morning just to have a look around with you? It would only take an hour," he asks me by phone, adding that he wants to bring a friend along. "We can get out there pretty quickly."

Of course I say yes. Margaret always told me that this was one of my worst habits. I can't say no when people make requests like this. She knew I liked to show off the ranch and help other people restore their land. Chap and his guest tell me they'll arrive in half an hour. Margaret, like me, was a people person. She never got frustrated or hurried. She also knew that I have never, ever given a one-hour show. That one-hour tour for Chap turns into a six-hour tour. These guys are interested, and they're eating it up. They're asking questions, getting out and walking around, listening to everything I tell them about grasses and trees and water. And, I'll admit it, I feed on their interest.

When we get back to their vehicle and they're saying goodbye, Chap's friend from Colorado has one more question for me. "Mr. Bamberger, this is all well and good, but what happens to all this when you are no longer around?"

I've already told him that I've established a foundation to receive the ranch and have recruited likeminded board members and placed numerous deed restrictions on the land. There will never be any restaurants, gift shops, or vending machines here. I don't even want a paved parking lot. But my answer to him is, "I'll tell you this; you'll never see any damn cellphone towers out here."

Ten days later, I receive a nice letter thanking me for the day and the tour. The letter closes with a note that each of the men is sending me a gift and that they're concerned I may not like it. Two days later, I get a call from Merrill Lynch. They've received two 100-share certificates for a New York Stock Exchange Company as a donation to our preserve. I cash in the shares and put sixty-two hundred dollars in the preserve fund. Then I look up the company. It turns out that these two men own more than twelve thousand cellphone towers. That's where they got the money to make the donation.

To this day, they contribute to Bamberger Ranch Preserve every year.

The Treasures of Hes' Country Store

One day while we are out exploring the ranch, David decides to show me an area he calls the "bird feeder." He is not talking about a seed-filled box on a pole in the yard. His version of a bird feeder covers a lot more ground and takes care of a lot more birds. He drives a few miles from the ranch house, pulls off, and we strike out down a trail. We cross a creek—David hops across like a much younger man, refusing a hand—then we pop out near an open field. We march toward a high fenced area planted with berries, grains, and flowers, creating an oasis of food for anything that might fly past. He explains that he set aside this spot to keep out deer and give birds a safe place to stop as they cross the ranch, one where they are safe from most predators, thanks to the fences.

Then he is back in the car, jostling down a gravel road, talking about the bat cave that perches on the highest point on the property or explaining that Miller Creek flows from a spring that rises from the ground here. He spits out the window and tinkers with the two pocketknives stashed in the cupholder of his pickup truck. He rolls on, to what he calls the "kiva," an old water cistern that he remodeled into a gathering spot. A gate has been cut into the cement wall with a rock saw, and a wooden door fashioned to fit. Inside the stone structure, forty-five kids can gather around a fire pit to toast marshmallows, or a group of friends can listen to someone play music.

And right then, like some kind of divine timing, the Bluebonnet glides into view. The flatbed trailer rolls to a halt in front of a white planked structure. A carved wooden cigar-store Indian stands out front, and a herd's worth of blanched deer antlers is nailed across the awning of the front porch. A white and red sign across the top reads "Hes' Country Store." David brightens and dashes over to meet the group, waving his hands and launching

David and Joanna sit on the porch of Hes' Country Store, 2017.
Photo by Pam LeBlanc.

into yet another of his famous stories. He wants to tell them about his mother.

⁓⁓

I'm out at the ranch when the phone rings. It's my mother, calling from Ohio. She tells me she needs to talk to me, and she's acting a little funny. I tell her to hold on, I need to sit down, but she says, "No, I can't talk on the phone. Don't you remember I'm still on a seven-party line?"

She wants to talk to me in person, so I arrange for her to fly to San Antonio. A few days later I drive down and pick her up. When we've unloaded and she gets settled in a bit, I notice that she's pacing around. She weighs ninety-two pounds and stands four foot ten inches tall and wears simple clothes—a pastel-colored button-down shirt and blue jeans that blouse at the bottom, like the Amish people who live near her.

I suggest we go sit on the patio, but she says, "Can't we go sit with your cows?" She loved animals and had never seen a big herd of cattle. The Amish people back home kept only one or two at a time. That worked just fine with me. I put her in my truck, and we drive down exactly to the inch where her country store now stands. We walk out into the pasture, and I lift her up and set her on the edge of one of the long feeding troughs where we spread out cottonseed cubes for the cattle.

Mom has never seen a massive number of cows, but in no time at all they start filing over, pushing in from all directions. They know they're going to get something to eat. One licks her leg with its long, fat tongue. That makes me a little nervous, because these are Brahman-type cattle, big animals that might accidentally knock my mom to the ground. Finally, the cows realize we don't have any food for them. They give up and start wandering away.

My mother looks around at the land, which seems to go on forever, with hills and trees and fields filled with grass blowing in the breeze. That's when she starts asking questions. "David, how big is this farm?" she says.

I tell her, "Mom, they call it a ranch here in Texas, not a farm." I'm egotistical and proud of my accomplishments, and I tell her I own more than five thousand acres.

"David, how many cows do you have?" I tell her I don't know, because it changes all the time, with some being born and sold all the time. She looks at me. She can't believe it. She's never known anyone with so much land or so many cows they didn't even know how many they owned. The people she knows in Ohio live in tiny houses. The wealthy ones own perhaps a hundred acres.

She says, "Let's see, you have that nice home in San Antonio. And, gee, I like this ranch house you have here."

But something about this is rubbing me wrong. I raise my voice. "Mom," I say. "Just what the hell is this all about?"

She meets my eye. "You look at me," she says, serious, "and you tell me you got all this and you did it

honestly," as if I'd robbed a bank or run drugs to get it.
She'd traveled fifteen hundred miles just to ask me that
question—she wanted to know if I had earned all this the
honest way. I assure her I've never done anything illegal
to get this land or buy these cows. Besides, I'm not all
that interested in money anymore. I don't plan to leave
this ranch to my children. I think it might mean more to
others.

She starts talking about how even with everything
I've got, she'll never be a burden on me. I try to quiet
her, and then she tells me, "I'll tell you something, David,
nobody's ever going to put me in one of those ware-
houses." She meant she never wanted to live in a nursing home. She goes on. "If you ever try to reach me and
you can't find me, look for me in my trees," she says. She
reminded me how as a little boy I'd followed her around
when she planted apple trees around her house. She
proudly tells me that she still got a few apples every year
from those old, half-dead trees.

I point across the road and show her this spot,
underneath the trees, where the country store now
stands. I tell her I'm building a log cabin. She tells me
she loves log cabins, like the ones tucked in the hills of
Ohio near where she lives. She wants to know why I'm
building one. I try to explain why I'm doing it. My attitude about so many things has changed. My philosophy
has changed. I'm really not interested in making money.
I want this ranch to be more than something some rich
guy bought and improved. Maybe it'll be a little museum.
Maybe just a gathering place.

"David," she says, "If you build that log cabin, would
you want any of my things?"

Five months later, after my mother has gone back
home, I get a phone call from Ohio. It's a neighbor, who
tells me, "Mr. Bamberger, you need to come up here.
Your mother has died." He says they hadn't noticed
her outside, working in her garden like she usually did.

They went over to look for her and found her beneath the apple trees. In one hand she held a pair of pruning shears, in the other a bouquet of wildflowers.

I know that when she woke up that morning, she knew she didn't have long to live. She had taken envelopes—she always sliced up used envelopes to use as scrap paper—and made notes for all the things she thought I might like to have here at the ranch. She made sixty-seven notes in all, each a little rectangle with a handwritten message about a particular thing: "This knife I bought for 10 cents when I was 12 years old," or "Your Uncle Alf made these chairs in Hartford City, Indiana, in 1892. They are very old." She didn't have tape, so she took a length of string and ran it through each note and attached it to the grater she used to shred cabbage and another to the wooden plunger she used to crush that shredded cabbage and make it into sauerkraut.

Hes' Country Store is stocked with antiques and memorabilia from David's childhood in Ohio, including this container of "vermin killer." Photo by Pam LeBlanc.

Another was fastened to a pair of scrapers used to remove hair from the hide of a slaughtered pig.

Today, all those things line the walls and shelves of Hes' Country Store. When visitors come to the ranch, they stop at the store, and I let them walk around, looking at the old housewares my mother gave me and other things—an old cannonball dug up on a property I once owned, a vintage tray of watercolor paints, a chunk of flint the size of half a brick, the edges worked into the rough shape of a hatchet head.

It's a sort of museum, a repository for things from my past, but also a way to remind schoolchildren and other young visitors that they, too, can do their own kind of conservation work. I want them to be the ones who protect their family's history and culture. I want them to go to their grandparents and ask them questions: What kind of clothes did you wear when you were my age? What did you eat for dinner? What kind of toys did my dad have to play with? It's worked, too. I got a letter from a ninety-two-year-old man whose granddaughter came here on a field trip. "My granddaughter never gave much of a hoot about me until she went to your ranch," the letter said. "Now she comes to see me once a week, with a clipboard and pencil, asking me all kinds of questions. Thank you." That's what Hes' Country Store is all about. My mother would be proud.

—⁓⁄⁞⁓—

An Alamo Relic

All kinds of things crowd the shelves at Hes' Country Store at Selah, where David has arranged relics salvaged from his childhood home alongside other assorted antiques. Rusty tin canisters that once held coffee share space with cast-iron skillets, yellowing photographs, scuffed glass bottles, and kitchen gadgets. When tour groups come through, David stands behind the kitchen counter and plays a game with the visitors. He pulls something off

David walks through Hes' Country Store, February 2017. Photo by Pam LeBlanc.

a nail where it hangs on the wall, a metal scrubber or an old tool. He raises it over his head and asks the group if anyone knows how his mother once used it.

"A potato peeler?" someone might suggest.

"A scrubber to clean pots?" someone else might guess.

Then David drops a hint: It is something used to make a snack you can buy at the grocery store (in Texas, anyway), he says, grinning a little. The crowd cannot figure it out. Surely that rusty currycomb-looking object was not used to make tortilla chips or Cheetos, was it? David finally gives in. This special scraper, he announces, once removed hair from the hide of a slaughtered pig. Past generations used it to make homemade pork cracklins— what today we call pork rinds. Mystery solved.

One winter day after one of those presentations, I wandered around the room with David, picking up old metal objects and turning over eighty-year-old bottles to see if I can still read the labels. Then I find something hidden on a shelf in a corner, looking for all the world like an ancient bowling ball without the finger holes or a dusty cannonball shot from a pirate ship. It is a little

David holds a cannonball he says was used in the Battle of the Alamo. Photo by Rodolfo Gonzalez.

bigger than a grapefruit and weighs a whole lot more. "That's a cannonball from Santa Anna," David tells me. "And I've got a story about it."

⚬⚬⚬

Back in 1959, I planned to build my first house on a vacant property across the street from Maverick Elementary School in San Antonio, which was built on the Maverick family's old Sunshine Ranch. Junk and brush clogged my old lot, and I recruited a non-English-speaking man to clean it up for me. I told him I'd pay him to do the work, and I'd also let him take any old iron he found there to sell as scrap. That was no small job. The man worked and worked and worked. At one point, he started to clear out the crumbling remains of an old barn that was falling to its knees. Just a mound of rotting boards and metal pieces remained of the structure, which had belonged to the Maverick family.

If you look up the history, you'll learn that Sunshine Ranch was part of an original Spanish land grant given to Samuel A. Maverick, who lived in San Antonio in the 1830s. Maverick went on to sign the Texas Declaration of Independence and at one point served as mayor of San Antonio. (He's also the man behind the word "maverick," used to describe an independent-minded person or steer.) Along the way, his family had acquired some of the cannons left in the ruins surrounding the Alamo. Those cannons were distributed among family members.

As my hired man cleared out the lot, he found a big piece of iron. He dug and dug and dug, but the chunk wouldn't budge. He went across the street to find the janitor at the school. "Brother," he said. "I need some help. Can you help me get this chunk of iron into the bed of my truck?"

The janitor went over and started to help the guy but pretty quickly realized what he'd uncovered was more than a hunk of metal from the barn. "I don't think you better sell this as scrap iron," he told the worker.

The janitor returned to the school to alert the principal. In a few minutes, she trotted across the street and announced that no, what the men have found is not scrap iron but something of historic value. She called the Witte Museum of San Antonio. They called the police, and someone sent out a wrecker. They proceeded to wench an entire cannon up out of the earth and take it back to the museum.

All that time, I sat at home with the flu. When my son David, who attended the school at the time, came home from class, he told me, "Dad, they found a cannon on our lot."

I was burning with fever and concluded David was suffering an even bigger fever than me. But about a month later, a newspaper story proved my son right. A picture of the cannon was plastered across the page with a headline that said, "Old Cannon Comes to Rest." That old chunk of "scrap metal" turned out to be one of Santa Anna's cannons, used in the Battle of the Alamo. I was so mad at myself for letting that cannon get away. But I talked to a lawyer friend, who explained a few things to me.

"One, you told the hired man he could have any iron he found," he said. "Number two, the Witte Museum now has it in its possession. Three, the Maverick family left it there. It was their personal property. Finally, in Texas, buried or newly discovered treasure belongs to the state. David, you're not going to get this cannon back, and what would you do with it if you did?" Well, maybe I would have put it in the front yard and hung my mailbox from it. But I got the point.

"You'd give it to the museum, wouldn't you?" the lawyer kept on. I kept my mouth shut. Still, my lawyer contacted the museum, which told him they'd give me credit for finding the cannon if I could prove the story. To prove it, I needed a sworn deposition from all the players—including the principal, the janitor, and the man who was clearing away the iron.

How do you find a day laborer in a city of half a million people? I drove up and down the west-side streets of San Antonio every evening for a month, and damned if one day I don't find his truck—and him. He isn't too comfortable going to a lawyer's office and giving his testimony, but eventually I was successful in getting everyone but the school principal to swear that the cannon was found on my property. The school principal didn't care too much for me, probably because my son in the sixth grade there once smarted off to her. I needed her deposition and she knew it, but before I could change her mind, she died.

So the museum kept the cannon, and I never got any credit for its discovery. I went back to my lot and eventually built my house there. And when I did, I found that cannonball. Did I tell the museum? Hell, no.

—⁓⁓—

Speaking to Catfish

When visitors pile onto the Bluebonnet, David hams it up. He knows exactly how to work it, too. I have seen it a dozen times. He stands at the front of the trailer, hanging on to the rail as the trailer bounces down the road. He dives into a story as the truck rolls down narrow ranch roads, pointing out creek beds or canyons or fields of grass along the way, that old tent-revival preachermanship coming out again as he shares the word of Mother Nature. The tour groups play right into his hands. They have come to Selah to learn about conservation and what they can do to improve their own small slices of the Texas Hill Country. But they have also come to get to know the Great Bamberger. And he never disappoints.

~\!/~

We built the catfish tank in about 1975 and made a pier, supported by concrete buttresses, that cut down the middle of it. We piped in water from a nearby spring, and when we filled it up, we had a six hundred–acre watershed. Now that we had a pond, I wanted to fill it with fish so we could drop in a line and go fishing. I went out and bought one thousand or so baby fish, each one smaller than the end of my finger. A guy brought them over in big plastic tanks, and I helped him dump them all into my pond. He told me I'd need to feed them, and he told me exactly what to buy at the feed store.

I drove over to the store and picked up a bag of fish food, kind of like you'd buy a forty-pound sack of dog food. Every day, I'd fill a coffee can with those pellets, walk out on that pier we built, and throw handfuls of fish food in there, raining it down like I was casting out seed to plant a field of grass. Those fish started to grow. Pretty soon they stretched as long as my finger. I threw out more food. They kept growing. Now they each weighed nearly a pound and measured a foot long. After a while I started to notice those damn fish were getting big. After a while they started to know when I was coming out to feed them. Fish underneath the water can sense the vibrations of a person walking down a pier. I'd walk out there to throw out food, the pier would quiver ever so slightly, and pretty soon the water would turn white with fish splashing around trying to get at it.

David still keeps a small herd of cattle at Selah. Photo by Pam LeBlanc.

This turned out to work pretty well when I'd drive people around the ranch. One day we got the Bluebonnet loaded up with a tour group, and we drove over toward the tank. Along the way, I announced to the crowd, "I'm going to talk to some fish." We pulled over next to the pond, and every eye was on me as I marched out there to the pier, then walked down it. I raised my hands up in the air. "Catfish, catfish of the Bamberger Ranch, come up and speak to these people," I hollered out, making sure I tapped my foot extra hard to create some good vibrations. The fish came boiling up out of the water, like water on a hot stove. They did exactly what I wanted. To the observer, it looked like they were answering my call. Someone back on the trailer shouted out, "He's God! He's God!"

A Crash Landing

David does not really have an airstrip at Selah, but some people apparently think he does. Ask him about it and he laughs, then sort of rolls his eyes. He has a story, of course. After he shared this one with me, I typed the words "Bamberger airstrip" into my smart phone, just to see what would happen. A link to a company that charters private jets popped up, noting that "Bamberger Ranch Airport is a local private jet airport located in Texas, United States, suitable for a variety of private jets." It is not.

And if you type the words "Bamberger Ranch Preserve" into the map feature on an iPhone, it will zoom you to the area just south of Johnson City, where you will see a dot for the ranch, and just a little north of it, a tiny airplane icon and the words "Bamberger Ranch Airport." And that is a bit of a stretch. Perhaps once you could land a plane there. But nobody in his or her right mind today would try to land a plane out on this hilly, tree-covered, rock-peppered stretch of the Hill Country.

~\|/~

I get a phone call one day back in the 1970s when I'm trying to develop a breed of cattle we called Grassmasters. This guy says, "Bamberger, I'm bringing a couple of people up to look at your cattle. I'll be there in about an hour." I tell him that will be fine, but he doesn't tell me how he's getting here. It turns out that he's planning to fly over, he's bringing two guests, and he thinks he's going to land his plane right here on the ranch. Our airstrip isn't really an airstrip at all, though. It's nothing but dirt and cows and a bunch of cow manure. Nobody uses it, and I had no idea at the time that it was included in some official book somewhere that lists the locations of airstrips all around the state.

So this guy flies to the ranch and starts to land his plane, but he's got a tailwind and he can't get his plane down. He realizes he's not going to make it at the last minute, so he pushes the throttle forward and tries to take it back up. The undercarriage catches some trees, and the plane gets snagged in the branches. The plane comes down, but not how the pilot had planned it.

All this time I'm somewhere else on the ranch and have no idea what's going on. Eventually I get back to my house because I'm going to meet this man, and an hour or two later, I hear a knock on my door. I'm thinking, "Hell, who's that? There's nobody out here." I go to the door and there's this guy, four or five teeth knocked out, bleeding like hell from his mouth. He tells me he's crashed his airplane and he's got two injured passengers. I go running down there, and we find the plane suspended in the top of a cluster of live oaks. I think the passengers got hurt more climbing out of the plane and falling to the ground than they did in the actual crash, but the net result was that the pilot sued me and the two passengers sued me and this thing goes all the way to court.

Pretty soon I've got lawyers and the Federal Aviation Administration crawling around out here. They showed me the book that includes a listing for Bamberger airstrip. According to the list, which I didn't even know about, my airstrip is 1,842 feet long, but it's really only 1,500 feet long, and there's no wind sock. I'm sued for failing to maintain a proper airport. Airport? My butt. Still, I have insurance. The case goes to a jury, and the lawyers for my insurance company come to me and tell me they want to settle.

"We're going to settle?" I ask, incredulous because I'm not guilty of anything. But against my wishes, they settle out of court. And then the jury comes out and announces that I'm not guilty, but the pilot is guilty of pilot error. All this, after my insurance company has settled the case for about fifty thousand dollars. I'm so mad I drop my insurance. Three months later, though, and I'm back on my knees, asking for coverage again. No other company will have me.

⁓⁄⁖⁚⁓

presentation that I presented at a booth at the San Antonio Livestock Show. We developed a mailing list of more than one thousand ranchers and put out a newsletter telling them how we were coming along.

For our breed, I came up with the name Grassmaster. What a hell of a name. Here was an animal that could eat grass and produce a fine lean steak. I partnered with some restaurants in San Antonio, and each year at stock show time I'd take a bull or a cow with a calf to the parking lot at those restaurants for publicity. The calves we produced from artificial breeding were born at 38 percent buffalo, but we didn't have much success breeding those animals. Not until we got down to animals that were 19 percent buffalo did we find enough fertility in the males. When that happened, I started to build a herd of Grassmasters. We went to College Station and started to bring professors out to Selah to show them what we were doing.

The university agreed to do some tests. The first tests focused on six of my Grassmaster calves that were born on the ranch, young yearlings. They were matched up with six control animals—Brahman-Hereford crosses from another ranch. The university operated on every one of them, cutting into their throats and inserting tubes into their esophaguses. Then they put a big bag on the cow, over its neck and across its back. Every morning they turned a valve. When the cow went out to start eating, nothing went into its stomach. It all went into that bag. After a few hours, they rounded up the cows and removed the bags. The students laid out everything the cow ate, including acorns and live oak leaves, which other breeds don't eat. My animals ate rougher forms of cellulose than the ordinary cattle. That was pretty good.

The university then asked me to fund another study, which I did. This time they took the same animals and hung a fecal bag on each one. They went through the same routine, only this time they fed the animals oats, wheat, and corn to fatten them up. Then they weighed the cows. The payoff came when the animals were slaughtered. They brought in all these muckety-mucks who look at cattle at auction and asked them to judge them while they were still alive. Then they slaughtered them. My animals came out with less fat and bone and more red meat, all the things that have to do with consumer health and rancher profitability.

I put the meat in butcher shops in Fredericksburg and San Antonio. I carried it myself in boxes to people's homes and sold it to them. Then in the late 1970s, I took a package of my meat to the grocery chain Whole Foods. They were really interested, but the reason they didn't go with me was this: They said, "We can't spend time promoting something when you only have the meat one month out of the year." I needed at least ten thousand Grassmaster cattle available for slaughter for any supermarket chain to take it as a product.

Our operation got some attention from big feed companies and breeder organizations that supported research. But Buddy wasn't enthusiastic about promoting it. I brought people to the ranch who were ready to lay money on the line, but Buddy wouldn't sell it to them or get very excited about. Then he retired. My new livestock manager wasn't interested in it. I couldn't do it alone. I had to call a halt to it. I calculate that I had spent more than half a million dollars on this project, and I was very disappointed in its failure.

~⁌~

A Nonnative Species Comes to Selah

As much as David talks about native grasses and restoring the land to the way it once was, one corner of Selah looks nothing like what you might have seen here five hundred years ago, because a herd of scimitar-horned oryx, a type of antelope once widespread across North Africa, lives there. During the 1970s, David served

A scimitar-horned oryx glows in the evening light at Selah, late summer 2017. Photo by Rodolfo Gonzalez.

on the board of the San Antonio Zoo and learned that zoos across America were struggling to replace certain species when they died because of the legalities surrounding the importation of animals. He wanted to do something about it.

Space is an issue at zoos, David explains one day, as we drive his old pickup truck into the section of Selah where the oryx live. The herd includes several spindly-legged babies, and we are trying to sneak up on them to get a closer look. They are not cooperating, so we park the truck and watch from afar. The animals look like they must look in the wild trotting across wide expanses of grass, the mothers protectively blocking our view of the young ones. Most zoos average less than twenty acres in size, David tells me. Most do not have room to sustain their own breeding programs. "It doesn't take much space if you're trying to save a snail darter, but how do you save an elephant?" he says.

He had a plan. He called his staff of experts together. The zoo community had started something called the Species Survival Program, he explained to them. The zoos worked together to share and breed animals, but only zoos could officially participate. David's staff put together a paper, which he presented to the Association of Zoos and Aquariums, offering to devote six hundred acres of his Hill Country ranch to the propagation of a species of their choosing. Experts from the association would teach the ranch staff how to manage the animals, and he would build whatever facilities were necessary.

David's plan was well received locally but stalled at the national level. "The debate was because they'd never put any of their animals outside a zoo. They couldn't believe that a bunch of cowboys down in Texas could handle what had to be done," he tells me now, as I watch the herd in the distance. Their ridged, slightly curved horns are so long that the animals look like they could tip over. The debate grew, and many were skeptical. Five members of the Association of Zoos and Aquariums visited Selah at the time to get a better idea of what David was doing at the ranch. They liked what they saw. Details were hammered out. Contracts drawn up. "It was the first time the Association of Zoos and Aquariums had entrusted genetic material to anybody other than another zoo," David says.

Members of the association settled on the scimitar-horned oryx because enough known genetic material existed in America and several other countries to start a breeding program. "You cannot save a species without knowing the genetic material," David says. "You have to know the parents, or you could get genetic abnormalities."

David traveled to Front Royal, Virginia, where the Smithsonian Conservation Biology Institute spearheaded its research programs. There, he witnessed the birth of twin oryx and signed the contracts, which ensured that nobody dumped surplus oryx at Selah and that only animals with known genetic material went there. The program nearly got off to a rocky start when a truck driver called him not long after the contracts were signed, saying he was on his way to the ranch with five oryx. "I said, 'Really? Who are you? I don't know anything about them,'" David says. He called the species coordinator he was working with, who told him he was not supposed to be getting any animals just yet.

"That didn't bode well for our program to save the species," David says. "These animals were not part of the species program. They had unknown parents and could not be used." Those illegitimate oryx were sent to a Hill Country ranch where the animals could be hunted, raising the ire of the animal rights community, which then picketed the zoo.

Eventually David received a batch of oryx, all with known bloodlines. Things settled into a routine. Whenever an oryx was born at Selah, workers tattooed its ear with identification information, which was then supplied to the zoo community. Each summer, he received a list of all transfers and breedings for the Species Survival Program. Some of the animals born and bred at Selah were sent to zoos around the country.

David was even instrumental in bringing an offspring of an oryx from Chad, which had been gifted to Fidel Castro of Cuba, to Canada. Abelardo Moreno, director of the zoo in Havana, Cuba, contacted David, telling him that he had two oryx that Fidel Castro had received from Muammar Gaddafi, the Libyan leader, as a gift after his troops had invaded Chad. He wanted to give them to David's program.

David wrote him back five times but never received a response. The government, David believed, had blocked his letters to Moreno. The species' US program coordinator suggested that Canada, which had maintained diplomatic relations with Cuba, make contact. Officials in Canada did and were successful in getting one oryx shipped to them. David then sent one of his oryx to Canada, where it was successfully bred with the Cuban animal. That, experts told him, brought in new genetic material that could extend the lifeline of the species by fifty years. "It was a home run," David says.

Because of the program's success, a group of people from the zoo community came to Selah to see what David was doing. At the time, David was still in the fried-chicken business. Instead of serving them traditional Texas barbecue, which they had been getting at every ranch they visited, David's engineers set up his fryers outside Hes' Country Store and cooked fried chicken. "You ever been around a bakery? That's the way it is around fried chicken," he tells me. "Here come my three big-ass buses. They pull up and everyone gets off and they smell this chicken and the place goes berserk. We feed 150 people. They're sick of barbecue because they've been in Texas for five days and now they're getting fried chicken and jalapeños. It's a wonderful, beautiful day."

After that chicken lunch, David loaded everyone onto flatbed trailers for the three-mile drive over to the oryx habitat. Along the way, they stopped at Madrone Lake, where David turned on his "rain machine" to show how grass slows runoff and allows moisture to soak into the soil. "What's that got to do with oryx?" he asked the crowd in typical showman fashion. "Gentlemen, what do oryx eat? Grass. This is to demonstrate what we've done on this ranch to make sure our oryx have an adequate natural food supply." The group drove on to the site, passing a sign that said "Sahara," all the way to special pens he had built to hold animals needing veterinary or other special attention. One zoo official asked how the crew filed the animals' hooves, something that had to be done weekly at his zoo. The Selah staff laughed. At

An oryx skull decorates the mantel of the guesthouse at Selah, where Pam stayed periodically while writing. Photo by Pam LeBlanc.

Selah, where the animals roamed in pastures like they do in the wild, their hooves did not need to be filed. It happened naturally.

As the oryx program continued, however, David faced steady criticism from animal rights groups, who were convinced he was selling oryx to ranches for private hunts. "We never did, period, even though we were offered as much as ten thousand dollars to hunt one," David says. "The animals belonged to us as a group. They belonged to the Species Survival Program, and the object of every species survival program is ultimately to restore the population back into the wild. The idea was to save this species from certain extinction."

Then, the Association of Zoos and Aquariums pushed David to take in more than the limit of 108 animals he had agreed to harbor. That many animals, he knew, would place too much stress on his ranch. "I said, 'I cannot tear down one form of conservation to build up another.' I spent a good deal of my life taking a worn-out piece of pastureland and turning it into grassland. I'm not going to let that happen." In 2011, David ended the oryx program, which cost him about thirty thousand dollars a year to support. Today he maintains a personal herd of forty or fifty oryx.

Saving the Snowbells

I love imagining a younger David, his blue eyes sparkling mischievously, dangling from the side of a rocky escarpment near the Devils River in Southwest Texas, harvesting seedpods from an endangered Texas snowbell. The plant grows there—on rocky cliffs and in drainage areas mainly along the Edwards Plateau—a defiant little shrub bearing light green leaves with silvery undersides that thumbs its nose at extreme heat and the need for much soil. In spring, clusters of dainty white, bell-shaped flowers appear on its slender branches.

David first learned about the snowbell when he received an award from the Nature Conservancy of Texas. The organization presented him with a plaque featuring a picture of the plant on it. Then, while volunteering at the Nature Conservancy's new property at Dolan Falls on the Devils River in the early 1990s, he saw snowbells blooming in the wild. He fell deeply in love. A Texas Parks and Wildlife Department employee sensed the romance and suggested that David take up the cause. He could, he noted, make a difference in the fate of the endangered plant.

"I took up the gavel and said, 'Hell, I could. I could help save that plant,'" David says. David ultimately spent more than twenty years working to save the snowbell, which was listed as federally endangered in 1984. He was determined to help this rare native Texas species make a comeback. David laughs about it now. "When I started the snowbell campaign, I didn't know how saving a plant that sounded so nice could get so tough," he says.

David knew he had to get private landowners involved, or the flowering plant, which can grow to a height of about fifteen feet, would disappear. He spent years cultivating relationships with his fellow ranchers, driving from ranch to ranch, knocking on doors and asking permission to crawl through canyons looking for this special shrub, which prefers steep cliffs near deep-cut waterways. Often, that ended with a door slammed in his face. At the time, most ranchers harbored suspicion when it came to the Endangered Species Act. Some called it a communist plot to take over private land.

It took David almost four years of chasing leads, trying to make friends, and tromping through ranchland, but little by little, he made headway. He even convinced some former critics of the Endangered Species Act of its benefits. Some of those same ranchers now proudly post signs on their gates to let others know they are recipients of the Lone Star Land Steward Award. David also gathered snowbell seeds and began propagating them at the ranch. He even built a greenhouse to assist in the growing process.

The US Fish and Wildlife Service learned of David's work and provided some funding for his project. They required him to record exact locations, using GPS, of where he collected the seed and where he planted the small plants he had raised. They also required him to place the plants he raised in the same watershed where he had collected the seed a few years earlier.

David and Steven Fulton would head to Edwards, Real, Val

Verde, and Uvalde Counties periodically, camping out or staying on area ranches and spending the days hiking down riverbeds, looking for snowbells clinging to cliff walls. David collected seeds from those plants, brought them home to propagate, then returned to South Texas to plant the budding shrubs. Scientists thought the plants grew best on cliff walls, but David believed they grew there only because livestock and deer could not reach them. He planted snowbells in pastures and river bottoms, then surrounded them with sturdy cattle panels to keep out domestic livestock and exotic species like aoudads that lived on many of the ranches.

Even late in life, David kept a finger in the project. In September 2017, at age eighty-nine, he and Joanna traveled to a ranch south of Sonora, where he delivered seed and planted five snowbell plants he had grown at his Blanco County ranch. He made a difference. In 1987, when the State of Texas listed the plant as endangered, only eighty-seven plants were known to exist, and almost all of them grew on private land. Today the snowbell is still listed as endangered, but its prognosis has improved. David and coworkers on the project have discovered more than 300 snowbell plants in Texas and planted at least 1,000 more, of which more than 640 have survived and are now blooming and producing seed. About fifteen hundred snowbell seeds are still stored in paper bags in a refrigerator at Selah, and David has provided seed to three Texas seed banks, as well as the National Arboretum in Washington, DC, where they are preserved.

꙳

Patty Leslie, a well-known botanist working at the San Antonio Botanical Garden, tells me one day about a Texas snowbell she knows that's growing on the grounds of the Texas State Capitol. She doesn't know exactly where it's growing, but that really doesn't matter. I figure I know enough about the plant by now that I can find it pretty easily. Plus, I need a new source of seed for my project.

I head downtown and start working my way around

the Capitol grounds, which are crisscrossed with chain-link fences due to a massive renovation project going on. I poke around outside the fences for a while and even try to squeeze through an opening before a uniformed state employee stops me and politely ushers me away.

Still, not a snowbell in sight. I start to walk back to my truck when I finally spot it—a tree loaded with beautiful flowers and plenty of seeds. I can't reach it, though. I need a ladder. No problem. I return the next day with a ladder slung over my shoulder and an armload of paper sacks. Pretty soon I'm climbing up that tree, sprinkling handfuls of seedpods as valuable as gold nuggets into those bags.

I don't notice at first, but someone's watching me from a short distance away. I get down to move the ladder, and he moves closer. I scurry up the tree again, but I sense him watching. I'm scared as hell but can tell he's unsure what to do. I look down at him, bag in hand, and say, with authority I certainly don't have, "Endangered species—all seeds needed to ensure its survival." He asks me what they are, and I proudly answer: "*Styrax texana*—commonly called Texas snowbell."

Fortunately, and this wasn't planned, I happened to be wearing a cap that says "Texas Parks and Wildlife Department." I think that's what saves my ass. The man walks on, and as soon as he disappears from sight, I disappear, too. I head back to the ranch, proud of myself for my great find. But the story doesn't end there. About a week later, twenty-five docents from the San Antonio Zoo come to the ranch for a tour. They're brimming with enthusiasm; they want to help us. "What can we do?" they ask. At this point I've got plenty of snowbell seeds and no idea of what to do next. I tell them about my plan to save this plant from certain extinction. I offer each of them six seeds and tell them to plant them in a Styrofoam cup with some potting soil. "Call me when they germinate, and I'll come pick them up and take it from there," I tell them.

Within a month, I'm getting calls. I have no idea

these snowbells are so easy to start. Here at the ranch, hundreds are sprouting. I'm excited about my success and collect nearly twenty small plants from my docent friends. I also enjoy some nice lunches and numerous desserts. Over time, we step these snowbells up into one-gallon containers. I line them up on a forty-five-foot stone ledge that runs from the fireplace to the patio door in the ranch house. I watch and nurture 106 snowbells. I'm so proud I haven't lost a single one.

Then David Braun, executive director of the Nature Conservancy in Texas at the time, comes for a visit. I know Braun because the Nature Conservancy has acquired a few thousand acres on the Devils River at Dolan Falls. That's where the largest known colony of Texas snowbells lives, and I've been down there to see them. He sees my neat row of healthy plants. "David, what are these?" he asks.

I'm so proud, I can't help myself from boasting a little. "You should recognize them," I say. "They're Texas snowbells." He marvels that he's never seen them grown in containers and offers me his congratulations.

A few weeks later, Andy Sansom, at the time the executive director of the Texas Parks and Wildlife Department, drops by for a visit. He spots my long row of snowbells and, like Braun, asks me what I've got growing. It's the same routine—I tell him I'm growing snowbells and graciously accept his compliments.

Then Nannette, a woman who helps me with my housekeeping, comes to the ranch house and admires my 106 healthy plants, which now stand fifteen glorious inches tall. She's overheard me bragging about how I skimmed these seeds right from the State Capitol. "Mr. Bamberger, I have one of these growing at my house," she says casually. I tell her she's certainly mistaken, that what she's looking at here is an extremely rare state and federally listed endangered species. "Well, I've got one," she insists.

All of this takes place as my relationship with Margaret is developing, so as the weekend nears, Margaret comes over and I tell her the story. She tells me that Nannette works part-time at the nursery in Johnson City and knows her plants. She suggests we drop by Nannette's house and take a look. I'm certain that Nannette doesn't have a Texas snowbell, and I don't want to lose such a good housekeeper by proving her wrong. But Margaret always wanted to be certain when it came to things in the natural world, so the following Saturday we head to Nannette's modest home in Johnson City. From the road her place doesn't look like much, but when we walk around back, we discover a little Garden of Eden.

Clearly, Nannette has the touch when it comes to flowers, shrubs, and trees. She leads us to the plant she says resembles mine, only instead of sprouting from a container, it stands five feet tall. Margaret quickly agrees it's the same plant as the 106 seedlings at my house and identifies it as a Chinese tallow—a most invasive and aggressive exotic tree. Have you ever seen a grown man cry? That's how I feel when I get this news. Needless to say, we remove all 106 of the Chinese tallows from my gallery and dump them, leaving a barren forty-five-foot rock ledge in my house.

〜ノⅠヽ〜

Digging for Artifacts

My family moved from Ann Arbor to Austin in December 1969, when I was five years old. My dad had been laid off from his job and landed a new one in Texas. He was my own personal rocket scientist and the one who instilled in me a sense of curiosity about the world. He couched the cross-country move as an adventure, and in my five-year-old imagination, I interpreted that as a move to the Wild West. Surely I would soon be riding ponies to school, playing in backyards overgrown with cacti, watching tumbleweeds blow down the road, and picking up arrowheads on every corner.

When my dad showed me how to fold two fingers down to form the "hook 'em horns" sign, I pictured kids at recess in a dust-covered schoolyard, hoisting their hands in the air—not in support of the University of Texas, because I did not understand the concept of college just yet, but because I knew I would be soon living among cattle with horns as long as grown men. I imagined them grazing on every empty lot in every neighborhood across the great state of Texas. None of that panned out, and I ended up going to Texas A&M University instead of UT, but David did have a role in making one of my long-held visions of life in Texas come true nearly half a century after we moved here.

One of the first times I met him, David walked me through what he calls the gallery of the ranch house, the long back room that had once been a porch but was later enclosed. The windowsill there stretches for forty-five feet along the back of the house and is more than a foot deep. Projectile points, fossils, rocks, and

David stands next to a tray of artifacts collected at a dig site on his ranch, May 2016. Photo by Pam LeBlanc.

other found-on-the-ranch bits of beauty cast off by Mother Nature fill nearly every square inch of that space, like an exhibit at a natural history museum.

When I first saw the collection, my eyes bugged out. As a kid freshly transplanted to Texas, I had dreamed about someday finding a single projectile point. And I had tried. After we moved to Texas, my dad drove us all over Central Texas in our yellowish-orange Volkswagen bus, exploring parks and tracking down obscure places of interest he had read about in a book. We hiked through cattle pastures in search of dinosaur tracks; we visited parks; we drove miles out of our way to see a car-sized rock precariously balanced on the side of a country road. We talked about the Native Americans who lived in Texas long ago, and I kept my eyes down on the ground, sure that if I searched long and hard enough, I would eventually turn up a perfectly shaped point.

It never happened. Not when we hiked in the little ravine at the end of our street in Northwest Austin, not when we tromped along creek beds or over ridges, not in our urban backyard, which my dad purposely left partly natural, with jagged chunks of limestone, little groves of cedar elms, and a big live oak, where he hung a rope swing.

When David told me he had found all those artifacts displayed on the windowsill on his ranch, I started dreaming all over again. "Spend a couple hours digging around in there, Pam, and you'll find something," David told me, referring to a special spot on Selah where many of the artifacts had been found. I left that day and did not hear from David for a year or so. Then, out of the blue, he called me and invited me out to the ranch. He wanted me to join him while he hunted for projectile points. I would have jumped in my car and driven out right then, but we set a date a few weeks later. I couldn't wait.

On the appointed day, Chris and I drove to the ranch house, where David and Joanna packed a hamper filled with sandwiches, chips, apples, and tea. We piled into David's old Toyota pickup truck, David behind the wheel, Joanna riding shotgun, along with me, Chris, and the dog, Cory, perched in the back. We liked riding back there because we could see out over the ranch while we bounced along gravel roads.

I asked David how he knew about this particular place on his land, and he explained that the man who had owned the property before him had pointed it out. Over the years, he had sifted through the dirt, turning up points that measured anywhere from an inch to five or six inches long. Some were finely shaped, others rough, as if someone had started making them, then discarded the work partway through. Many were chipped or broken.

We parked the truck at the site, not far from a creek, and David showed us around. Years earlier, he explained, he had tried to raise the interest of researchers at local universities. After repeated tries, no one seemed to care much. He told me, with a hint of embarrassment, that he had finally enlisted the help of one of the ranch hands to dig, with a backhoe, two parallel trenches, each about three feet deep, so he could take a look.

He knew that archaeologists would raise eyebrows at his unscientific methods. We stepped into the trenches—David and I in one, Joanna and Chris in the other. David handed us each an old trowel and showed us how to pick away at the dirt and

Chris LeBlanc pets Cory while Joanna and David finish a picnic lunch at the dig site at Selah, May 2016. Photo by Pam LeBlanc.

rock along the edge of the trench. We went to work. As I gently plucked out egg-sized stones and brushed away clots of dirt, David regaled me with stories. (I did not know it at the time, but he wanted someone to help him tell those stories, which is how this book happened.)

I am not sure who found something first. Probably it was Joanna. It usually was. Drawn by a flash of smooth gray flint in the dirt, she pulled out a point that made me swoon. But also, an hour or so into our adventure, I uncovered a rough-looking piece of flint, a little smaller than the palm of my hand, that had been chipped into what looked like a scraping tool. It may as well have been a chunk of gold. I examined each nick and notch on that bit of flint, thinking about the person who had made it so long ago. Maybe a tribe had gathered here, and some of the more skilled craftsmen were trying to teach the younger ones how to make tools.

David called the place a midden, a sort of domestic trash heap. Maybe this was where people tossed projectile points that were not up to snuff, or broken, or tools they no longer used or needed. We talked about it and wondered aloud what those people looked like, what they had been doing that day, and how their handiwork had ended up hidden under heaps of dirt and charred stones.

David, a glass of wine in hand, uses a trowel to scrape away dirt in a dig site at his ranch, April 2018. Photo by Pam LeBlanc.

As David and I worked, the discarded rock and dirt that we scraped from the walls started piling up in the trench behind us. He got some buckets, and we began filling them with the rubble. We hauled those buckets over to a pile, emptied them out, and filled them again with rubble from the trench. David and I made a much bigger mess than Joanna and Chris. And after a while, Chris came over to rake up behind us, using a shovel to scoop out the rocks we were leaving in our wake.

Over the course of the morning, we found a handful of items, some unfinished or broken, but one or two in nice shape. With every find, a yelp would sound and an arm would rise triumphantly from the pit. After a few hours, someone called for a break. We climbed out of the trenches, arranged our finds on the picnic table down by the site, and compared them to the points listed on a handy identification poster that David had laminated and hung there. We hovered over a nearby table, too, where other friends of the ranch who had gone hunting in the trench had left

Pam shows off a projectile point she found in the dig site at Selah. All projectile points found at the ranch stay there. Photo by Chris LeBlanc.

some of their lesser finds. Even that stash held what looked like treasure to me—bits of flint that had been worked by long-ago hands, shaped rocks that might have been used to scrape animal hides, even pieces of broken points.

The rule here was this: If you found it here, leave it on the ranch. Or give it to David to display at his home or at the ranch's education center—not for him to covet, just to keep them in a safe place, where others could see them.

A picnic always accompanied our "dig days." Once, David loaded an ice chest full of hot dogs, and when we got to the midden, he positioned an old tilling disc from a tractor over a makeshift grill and lit a fire. He cooked up beans and hotdogs in that contraption. As we ate them there at the picnic table, the warm Texas sun heating the backs of our necks, they tasted better than filet mignon.

I wished my dad could be there, too, because he had always felt the same way I did. He would have wanted to hold a point in his hand, roll it over, think about the person who had made it, who that person had loved and fought with and admired, who his friends were, what his daily life was like, what made him happy, and what he had eaten the day he made that point (probably not hot dogs cooked on a tractor blade). Chris and I visited the midden with David and Joanna three or four more times over the next year, and every visit turned up a point or a scraping rock. Once, I found one made of mustard-yellow-colored flint; another time Chris found one streaked in red and white. I carried them down to the creek, where I dipped them in clear water to rinse off the dirt. We always left them with David, where we could admire them anytime we visited.

The Bats Emerge

On a Friday night in early September 2017, David invites me and my husband out to Selah. We stay in the guesthouse and drive over to the main ranch house for dinner, which he declares will begin promptly at 6:11 p.m. (David loves to set arbitrary times for meetings.) He and Joanna grill up what he proudly calls "bean burgers." David's not vegetarian, though, and the burgers are not a new option at a trendy Austin restaurant that caters to nonmeat eaters. They're regular ground beef hamburgers (sometimes with venison from the ranch mixed in), spread with refried beans, then topped with crunched-up Fritos corn chips, picante sauce, and a dollop of guacamole. David plates the burger with the beans already crowning the patties; he wants to make sure you get the right ratio.

We settle in, enjoy dinner on the back porch, and let the sun drop in the sky. Then we pile into our pickup truck and make the ten-minute drive to David's very own, human-made bat cave, which he calls a chiroptorium. (His son David K. contacted three dictionary makers to request that they list that word, and they told him to prove that credible scientists accept the term. He submitted evidence, but so far the term has not appeared in a dictionary.)

The bats have not started to emerge yet, so David invites Chris to go take a look inside the cave. Even from across the road, we can smell the pungent aroma of guano. The two men tie bandanas around their mouths and noses and plunge ahead. I dash after them, holding the hood of my jacket over my face to keep me from passing out. We step just inside the mouth of the cave, and David, who in the 1980s served on the board of Bat Conservation International, a nonprofit organization based in Austin that works to protect the flying mammals, pulls out a flashlight. He flashes the light quickly around the garage-sized room. The nightly exodus is clearly about to begin. The bats are swirling like an old Warner Brothers cartoon of a Tasmanian devil.

A few fly toward the entrance. More follow. It is the first time I have watched the start of a bat emergence from inside a bat cave, much less a human-made bat cave, and I am pretty sure I will either get smacked in the face by a dozen or more furry little mammals or make some Mexican free-tails very angry. We hustle out after a few seconds so we do not further disturb the phenomenon. (David does not normally walk into the cave; he is protective of the animals.) Over at the picnic table, we pour a glass of wine and watch our own private performance, which officially begins at 7:15 p.m.

Bats emerge from the chiroptorium at Selah, summer 2017. Photo by Pam LeBlanc.

For the next twenty-six minutes, a dark ribbon of bats uncoils and snakes across the rose- and gold-colored sky, moving and twisting like a long rope held at either end by a couple of people snapping it back and forth. We are experiencing not just the sight of half a million Mexican free-tailed bats heading out for a night of insect foraging, but also the sound of hundreds of thousands of tiny flapping wings, a drumbeat that marks the approaching nightfall.

⁓⋎⋌⁓

I got interested in bats after watching them emerge from Bracken Cave near San Antonio. I decided I wanted a bat cave at Selah. I bumped around the idea with scientists I knew. No one was sure that if we built a manmade cave any bats would move in. Lots of people laughed at the idea. I decided to build it anyway, and bulldozers plowed up earth and dug out space on the side of a carefully selected canyon. Then we used rebar and concrete to build a three-chambered structure that looked like an upside-down swimming pool.

A few newspaper writers around the state heard about the project and called to talk to me about my latest (possibly harebrained) project. I answered skeptical questions and described my plans. One reporter ended the conversation with the question, "What are bats good for?" to which I responded, "I'll tell you this. You could come out here all day and run around naked and you wouldn't get bitten by a single mosquito."

That quote, of course, made it into print, and mosquito-hating readers from around the country took note. My phone rang. Nudist colonies called, people plagued by bugs called, and one woman from Minnesota, which apparently has a voracious population of biting insects, opened her letter with the comment, "I read with pleasure your quotation. How does one go about participating in such frolicking?"

Early on, it looked like the skeptics had been right after all. I checked frequently, but the bats hadn't discovered the cave—or if they had, they didn't think it was worth moving in. Three and a half years after we built the bat cave, a journalist from San Antonio who had written about the project when it began called back, perhaps a little sarcastically, to ask me how many bats were living in my chiroptorium.

"I said, 'I don't know, but each one is costing me five thousand dollars,'" I cracked.

To which the reporter replied, "You don't have any bats, do you?"

That conversation seemed to trigger the bats to stand up for me. The next day, bats began flooding out of the cave when I went up there to check on the status. They were coming out so thick you couldn't believe it. I started crying. I immediately called a bat expert I knew at Boston University. He told me not to get my hopes up, that sometimes a migrating group of bats stops for a night or two. The bats might never return.

But I thought they would. I called a TV weather forecaster I knew in San Antonio and invited him to come out and film the bats emerging the following day. He came out and got some footage that the TV station aired on the same day that the article by that reporter ran in the San Antonio newspaper, under the headline "Bamberger's Folly." I was vindicated.

⁓⁄ ⏐ ⬎⁓

The Family Picnic at Selah

Every spring, Selah swings open its gates for the annual Family Day and Picnic. David had been telling me about it for weeks, but I had never been, so Chris and I marked it on our calendars. David also gave me an extra invitation and asked me to share it with someone who would appreciate it. I knew just the person. My friend Tammy Russell, a speech pathologist in Austin and single mother who had spent years fostering children with histories of abuse or neglect, had recently adopted three siblings—a boy and two girls, ages five, six, and seven at the time. She was also fostering a fourth, a four-year-old girl who she planned to adopt. They accepted the invitation, and on the appointed day, Tammy loaded the family into her car for the hour-long drive to Selah from Austin.

The 2017 picnic marked the thirteenth at Selah. It was a big day at the ranch, sunny and warm, with lots of activities for children. They could soar over the grass on a short zip line or hunt for fossils in the dirt. They could ride in a hay-covered flatbed trailer to a special corner of the ranch to see dinosaur tracks. Up at the main center, they could make nature-themed arts and crafts projects. Or they could walk down to Madrone Lake and learn how to use a rod and reel to cast a lure. They could hike and ramble and play in the great outdoors—something Tammy's kids had not had much opportunity to do in Austin.

David hosted the picnic because he wanted to expose kids — especially kids like Tammy's, who had not had much experience in the outdoors—to nature. He wanted them to learn to love and appreciate the land as his mother had taught him. I could relate to that. When I was growing up, my family camped regularly. We loaded up our Volkswagen bus with a giant canvas tent, the trusty Coleman cooler and camp stove, and packs of hot dogs and Tang, and visited Bastrop State Park and Enchanted Rock State Natural Area, Inks Lake State Park and McKinney Falls. My dad orchestrated the tent setup, and we arranged cots inside our bright blue shelter. My mom made breakfast, toast topped with orange slices and brown sugar, cooked on the grill. We washed it down with Tang, just like the astronauts did in the 1960s.

My father especially instilled in me a love of adventure that kept growing as I got older. I knew from experience that getting away from the house made me feel free. But many families do not have that background and would not know what to do with a fishing rod. Or a ranch to explore. Bamberger's picnic gave them a taste of that—and if David's idea worked, it would also instill in the next generation a sense of why it is important to take care of the land. The family-day event was a fundraiser, too, and picnickers could buy native plants to take home and grow on their own. They could bid on items in the silent auction, many of them handmade by ranch staffers and others donated by the community. Money raised from the sale of artwork, bird houses, wooden benches, books, and other items would help fund future educational programs for children.

When Chris and I got to the ranch, we headed straight to a covered tent, where biologist Jared Holmes, the ranch's education and outreach coordinator, had set up a dozen or so glass aquariums to display some of the snakes in the collection he kept locked up in the garage of the guesthouse where I stayed when I visited. (Yes, I thought more than once about what would happen if somehow the snakes all broke out and slithered their way into the bedroom where I slept just fifteen yards away.) Jared had collected almost all of them here on the ranch and knew everything about them. He was busy explaining the difference between nonvenomous rat snakes and vipers to some curious onlookers.

There were birds, too, from a nearby animal rehabilitation center. I stared an owl right in the face and met a hawk, before downing a plate of chicken fajitas served up by volunteers from the Bexar Grotto Cavers, a chapter of the National Speleological Society. David knew the cavers from his days working with them at Bracken Cave near San Antonio, home of the largest population of Mexican free-tailed bats in the world—more than fifteen million of the flappy little mammals. They volunteered to serve lunch every year at the picnic.

We settled in at a table for lunch and noticed Tammy, her flock of tiny kids in tow, all of them looking wide-eyed and a little apprehensive. They had made a few short school field trips to urban farms or nature centers in Austin but had never visited a place like this, where nobody cared if they got dirty or ran fast or made noise.

"To get in the car and drive an hour away and go up these windy roads and then, boom, here is this preserve," Tammy told me later. "It's not something we have at our fingertips. It's not something you'd think you could have access to, living in Austin or any city. That you can drive an hour away and see so many trees and so much water." The experience reminded her of the importance of setting aside open land and left her with an admiration for the work taking place at Selah.

"What a mission," she said. "To decide that you would commit your life to preserving that land is just amazing to me." And it was fun. Her children stood, for the first time, in footprints made long ago by real dinosaurs. They searched for small fossils next to a pasture. They learned about nature from ranch staffers and volunteers who took the time to chat with them one on one. And down at the lake, someone placed a rod in their hands for the first time, and they tried to cast into the water.

"There were so many kids down there trying their best," she said. "All of mine tried. My oldest was the only one who succeeded in casting his line more than a few inches in front of them. They all tried a few times. Casting was definitely hard for them, as was being patient to wait to see if they caught anything."

Lots of people had come to the ranch that day, but it did not feel that way to Tammy and her family. "It didn't feel like that many people because everything was so detail oriented and special," she said. "It was just the time everyone was taking." Tammy realized later just how much of a hit the experience had been. For an entire week after the picnic, Tammy's kids kept recreating some of the scenes from Selah. They set up a pretend fossil dig, they gave talks, and they reminisced about fishing. "That to me is always a sign," she said. "For these guys, that's what makes you know that it was cool." She summed up the meaning of the day in a letter to David:

Dear Mr. Bamberger and family,

I wanted to write to thank you for the amazing experience my family and I had on Sunday. We enjoyed every single bit of the time we spent on your ranch. My kids were able to step in dinosaur prints, do crafts to their hearts' content, eat a cookie as big as their faces, zip line, fish, and more. These are opportunities that my kids have not previously had access to and I am so grateful for the experiences your Family Day provided.

What amazed me most about the Family Day was that—despite having almost 500 people on your ranch— YOUR family was available for ours. We ate lunch with your newest member, Sarah, and found fossils with Jared. I am pretty sure a Bamberger from San Antonio was the man who put a fishing rod in my son's hand for the first time ever and taught him to cast (or try to, at least). We ended up on a hayride with one of your sweet little ranchers who will be in kindergarten next year, and we ended our day chatting with "the" Mr. Bamberger on the way to the car. If this is not a good representation of what family is, I am not sure what would be.

Since Sunday, we have done nothing but fly kites, see if our flowers are growing (not yet), mourn the loss of peanut butter pine cones to the squirrels, and pretend to give presentations to each other about dinosaurs, snakes, and fishing.

Our experience with you will last far beyond the hours spent at your home. Thank you so much for the memories and education you have given us.

Tammy Russell

Sharing Stories in Front of the Fireplace

David popped by the guesthouse one afternoon while I was holed up there writing. He sat down at the table across from me, and after we had gone over some stories we were working on, he invited me and Chris, who was planning to drive over later from Austin, up to the ranch house for dinner the next night. I agreed, of course, because you never knew if David was going to unveil some new gem of a story. And dinner at the Bams', as Chris and I called it, with its window-lined gallery and brick fireplace big enough to roast a feral hog, could turn into a mood-altering experience.

David and Joanna share a kiss above Madrone Lake, late summer 2017. Photo by Rodolfo Gonzalez.

David told me Joanna was cooking pizza, and he promised that I would rapture when I tasted it. (A lot of rapturing happens at Selah. Everything is the best, the most amazing, the most beautiful.) Chris and I headed out a few minutes early the next night so we could swing by Madrone Lake on the way. In the two days since my arrival, the first cold front of the season had swept through, and overnight the lacy green fringe of the cypress leaves that lined the lake had been dipped in what looked like orange and gold wax. I loved fall and the way the trees shrugged off their summery green wardrobes and traded them in for something more serious. And in Texas, where summer brings day after day of temperatures in the hundreds, fall comes as a relief. We stopped to admire the color, then drove up to the ranch house, where David and Joanna swung open the door and ushered us in.

David loves to make things just right, and he had set the scene like he was staging a Broadway play. He swept us into the living room with a flourish and lit a fire just as we rounded the corner. A pair of iron caissons, with a couple of horse shoes big enough to fit an elephant welded to their bases, stood at the front of the cavernous brick fireplace. David extended a lighter, and suddenly flames were licking up a pile of firewood and ball moss that crackled like popcorn and created a waterfall of fire.

Joanna put the pizza in the oven as David and Chris pulled chairs around the fireplace. It felt good just to sit there, knowing temperatures were going to drop into the thirties in a few hours. Chris poured the wine, and I soaked it in—the warmth of the fire, the coziness of the room, and the smell of baking pizza. And then the stories came, like they always did.

I asked about David and Joanna's recent trip to South Texas to plant Texas snowbells, and he started chuckling. He did not tell us about planting the endangered plants he had spent his whole life working to preserve. He did not launch into a description of the ranch where they stayed during their visit. He wanted, instead, to tell us about a convenience store in Rocksprings, not far from the Devils River, where they stopped to fuel up the car he and Joanna and another couple were driving.

David decided to go into the little store and pick up some

hard cider for the two couples to sip while sitting on the porch at the end of the day. He carried the alcoholic cider up to the counter, and then, believe it or not, the clerk asked for his identification card. She needed to know if he was old enough to legally buy booze. That ticked off David. This was nothing like some clueless guy at the counter trying to flatter a fifty-something woman by asking her to show her ID card, then saying, in mock disbelief, "No, that can't be." This clerk was serious, and she had apparently been told to card Every Single Person who came in to buy booze. She would not bend the rules for some old man.

"You don't think I'm eighteen?" David asked her, fingers directed at his eighty-nine-year-old face (or some of them, anyway, since one of his arms was restrained in a sling from a recently broken shoulder, sustained while gathering leaves to tuck into the year's Christmas cards).

Someone noted that the drinking age is actually twenty-one, like it might make a difference in this specific case. Honestly, looking at David, you cannot believe he is eighty-nine. But he is certainly not eighteen, or twenty-one, or even fifty anymore. Yet the clerk remained firm. She needed that ID before she would hand over the booze. David stormed out of the store, flipping the clerk a center finger as he hustled out the door, nary a bottle of cider in hand. His outrage still shined through as he related the story to us.

The fire continued to crackle, and Cory shifted position a little on his dog-sized bed on the other side of the sofa. David mentioned another trip the couple recently took, this one to Dallas, where they attended an awards banquet to honor him for his environmental work. Joanna got seated next to one of the wealthy Fort Worth Bass brothers, and the two bonded, David says, over wine. I asked Joanna what Mr. Bass had to say about wine, and Joanna begins to tell a story.

"I've never told you about the 1982 wine?" she asked, incredulous.

David usually got the glory for weaving stories. A practiced artist, he knew just when to pause for effect and just when to roll with it. Yet Joanna was a master, too, when given the chance. When her husband was still alive, she said, and the couple lived in Canada, he liked to indulge in fine whiskey. Joanna, back then, drank cheap wine. She is not exactly proud of that, but at the time it did not matter much. Until one day, in 1981, when she decided it was time to start enjoying a little of the finer things in life.

She set out for Rochester, New York, to one of the country's largest wine importers, with two thousand dollars to spend to stock her cellar. She told the wine importer that she liked Bordeaux. Instead of buying wine that had already been bottled, though, he suggested that she buy some "future" wine. She decided on ten cases of French wine that had not been bottled yet. She paid the bill and drove back to Canada. When the wine was bottled and shipped to the warehouse a few years later, Joanna headed back down to pick up her allotment and bring it back home to Canada. (How she got that wine across the border is a whole other story.)

She broke into a few of the bottles over the next decade or so, but the wine took a while to mature, and some of it tasted better than the rest. Mostly she held on to it, and when she and her husband eventually moved to Texas, they brought the wine with them. In Texas, a few years later, Joanna befriended the owner of a wine shop on the outskirts of Austin. They got to talking, and she shared with him that she had a stash of 1982 Bordeaux in her cellar. That piqued his interest. The next time Joanna went to his shop, he asked her about that wine and if she might be interested in selling him a mixed case. She brought it in, and he disappeared in back to sort through the bottles. When he returned, he offered her two thousand dollars for the single case, the same amount she had originally paid for ten cases. That wine she had purchased, sight unseen, turned out to be a good investment. Experts later described it as the best wine produced in the Bordeaux region of southwest France in the past century. It had grown tenfold in value. And Joanna was sitting on cases of it.

The rest of that stash of wine was mostly gone by now, some of it poured for special occasions, some given to her son as a special gift. We set down our glasses. Joanna ducked into the kitchen to get the pizza, and David and Chris moved a table in front of the fireplace so that we could eat by firelight.

6

David and Friends

If left to David, the winter holidays would probably stretch well into spring, and possibly even summer. Drop by the ranch house in January, or even February, walk out into the back gallery, where the dining room table is set up overlooking the hills, and you will find hundreds of Christmas cards hanging from a string along the back window. After checking to make sure mine was there among the others one day (it was), I asked David why he kept them up for so long. That made both Joanna and David chuckle. David wanted to leave them up year-round. Joanna thought that was stretching it a bit. She had to lay down the law. David, she said, would be required to remove the cards by July 4, halfway to the next Christmas. David, who loves Christmas, gave in.

When Christmas Arrives by Train

David's mother, Hes, died in 1979. At her funeral, people told him many heartwarming stories about her. But he especially liked this one about the pines she planted.

~\⁄~

Sometime after Donna and I left for Texas, Mom learned
of a government program that was planting pine trees
on fallow land not suitable for farming. As a result of her
inquiry, a soil conservation biologist made a site visit to
explain the program to her. The pine trees were available
for free, but the landowner had to share the cost of the
planting. In the future, the biologist said, the trees could
be harvested as Christmas trees—and much later for
wood pulp. Mom signed up, and with the program's help,
she placed two hundred little pine trees in the ground in
neat rows.

You couldn't really call them trees yet, because they
stood less than ten inches high. At first, you could barely
see them through the heavy grass and brush, but she
visited them so regularly she wore a trail from her house
to the place they were planted. She was watching them
grow, and in a way, we were too. During our annual trip
to visit her with our three kids in the 1950s and 60s,
she'd lead us down that well-worn path to admire her
pine trees, which now stood out above the grass and
other growth.

Those trees eventually grew to four or six feet tall,
the perfect size for Christmas. Now Mom liked young
people with children, and she let it be known that if you
were parents with small children, you could come to her
property and, as a gift, select a pine tree for Christmas.
You had to bring along your own bow saw, or whatever
you needed to cut down whatever tree you selected, and
you couldn't just run out to her place and grab a tree.
You had to bring your children. Mom, of course, knew
what that experience would mean to kids.

That first year, at least eight or ten families took Mom
up on her offer. She'd lead the parents, children in tow,
down her well-worn path into her beloved pine forest.
They'd walk up and down the rows, the kids singing
and skipping, and together they'd pick out the tree they

wanted. The father would always kneel down in the grass with his saw to cut the tree down. When the tree fell, everyone cheered. Then, together, they'd carry the tree up to Mom's little house, a distance of about the length of two football fields. They'd lash the tree onto the roof of their car, or squeeze it partway into the trunk, and off they'd go.

Mom just delighted in helping those young families get their Christmas started. One year, I got a letter from her, saying, "Don't you buy a Christmas tree. I'm going to send my grandchildren one from right here in Ohio." And pretty soon, those pine trees of hers started making the trip all the way down to Texas. Here's how it happened. Mom would grab one of her bow saws (you can see them in Hes' Country Store at Selah), go down into that pine forest, pick out a tree, and crawl down underneath it. She was only four feet ten inches tall and weighed just ninety-two pounds, but there she was, pushing a bow saw back and forth until the tree finally came down. Then she pulled it out and dragged it away from her pine forest to her house.

With a ball of cord, starting at the top of the tree, she drew each branch up close to the trunk, and wrapped a length of cord around it, tying it into place. She'd turn the tree over, tie down a few more branches, and make her way until every branch was wrapped tight against the trunk. When she finished—and I'm sure it took her at least two or three days—she somehow got that tree into her car.

Back then, there was no such thing as UPS or FedEx shipping. Instead, she took the tree to the nearest Railway Express station. She'd tell the person working at the station that she wanted to send the tree all the way to San Antonio. I'm sure none of them had ever heard of someone shipping a Christmas tree to Texas, but they helped her out.

We'd get a postcard, letting us know our Christmas

tree would arrive at the Railway Express station in San Antonio on a certain day—usually four or five days after she'd taken it to the station. Donna and I would gather up our three kids and head down to the station. My kids loved it. They responded just the way those kids had when my mom let people pick a tree from her farm.

We'd take that tree home, use a pair of scissors to cut all the cord wrapped around it, little by little, and work to spread the branches back out. By Christmas day, we had the prettiest tree you could imagine. For three years in a row—until those pines grew too big for her to handle—Granny Hes sent one of her trees to us, and my kids looked forward to it. Not many grandmas did that. She wanted to be as much a part of our Christmas as she could from fifteen hundred miles away.

~/\~

A Trip to the Christmas Tree Lot

Every holiday season for nearly half a century, David worked the Christmas tree stand for the Alamo Heights Optimist Club in San Antonio. He would drive down from his ranch and pitch in, helping families pick out the perfect holiday tree, carrying it to their car, and tying it down for the trip home. And he could not resist putting his salesmanship skills to use at that stand, either. But in October 2017, he broke his shoulder while gathering fallen leaves to tuck into his annual Christmas card, and for the first time in forty-four years, he would not be able to work the stand. But he did not skip the tree business entirely that year, despite the broken shoulder. One Saturday in early December, two days after a surprise snowfall had sifted an inch of snow across the ranch, David, Joanna, Chris, and I arranged to go down to San Antonio to experience the tradition in person.

"It's a scene straight out of *Gasoline Alley*," he told me before we headed down. (I had to look it up; *Gasoline Alley* was a comic strip by Frank King, launched in 1918. It was also the first comic strip in which the characters aged at the same rate its readers

David examines a tree at the San Antonio tree stand where he volunteered each Christmas, December 2017. Photo by Pam LeBlanc.

did, so a baby dropped on the doorstep of the original main character's home grew into a man who enlisted in the US military, married, had kids, and even faced a midlife crisis years later.)

We parked around the corner from the lot, located near the intersection of Broadway and Austin Highway. As soon as we walked in the gates, before we even sucked in a lung full of that delicious pine-scented air, two young guys minding the stand just about freaked out. "Mr. Bamberger!" one of them shouted out and raced over to clasp David around the shoulders. Then the young man wheeled around, announcing to anyone within earshot, "This is a celebrity! The founder of Church's Chicken right here!"

David swelled with pride. He had been nervous, he told me later, that none of the people he had worked the stand with would be there. He held court for the next thirty minutes, basking in the

In December 2017, David walks down the aisle of the tree stand where he once volunteered. Photo by Pam LeBlanc.

glow of attention and sharing stories about the good old days at the tree stand. The two young men—Shane and Brian—told me they started working the stand in 2006, after the father of a basketball teammate enlisted their help in doing some heavy lifting at the tree lot. They came back year after year, matching sturdy green trees with eager families. In the years they worked with David, he told them stories (of course) and shared advice about life—what is important, what is not, what to focus on, what not to get stressed out about.

That is when I learned about "Discount Dave." David knew a thing or two about making a sale, whether it involved vacuum cleaners or fried chicken or noble firs. "The man could sell a ketchup Popsicle to a lady wearing white gloves," Shane told me. "He really could."

David never let anybody walk away from the stand without a tree—instead, he just cut them a deal. "Hey, today I'm offering trees at thirty percent off, just for you," he barked. The guys explained this to me as we walked down rows of trees, stacked high, breathing in the aroma of Christmas. David pulled out a couple of trees to demonstrate his tree knowledge. Noble firs, he said, are the best. Their branches are separated enough to hang ornaments, and they are shaped just perfectly. He twirled one around, like he was dancing with a woman in a lush, needle-covered skirt.

Then we walked over to the old travel trailer, which served as the checkout booth and headquarters for the tree lot. David was right. It came straight from the pages of a *Gasoline Alley* strip—old, retro looking, rounded at the edges, with an array of stuff like metal tree stands, evergreen branches, and a sign that said "Thanks to you, we've been here a long time" leaning against it. We stepped inside, and David pointed out how years earlier they had refitted the trailer, installing an honest-to-God booth from a Church's Chicken store inside it and making a stand where the

David in the trailer where the volunteers ring up Christmas trees. Photo by Pam LeBlanc.

money box was stored. Cozy and comfortable, this was where the workers came to take a break or ring up a sale.

Then David flipped open the notebook where the workers kept records. He ran his fingers down the rows of numbers, calling out the earnings for each day and flipping back to check records from previous years. His finger stopped and tapped on the row of figures from earlier in the month. Just a week earlier, the stand had recorded its biggest day in history, selling $9,713 worth of Christmas trees. "If Discount Dave had been here," he laughed, "they'd have broken ten thousand dollars. Did I ever tell you what I'd do?" he said. Well, no. Not yet. He chuckled at the memory of what he was about to tell me.

—᠁—

The trees we sold at the Alamo Heights Optimist Club tree lot all looked about the same—green and nicely shaped, with branches for hanging lots of ornaments. When I arrived for my shift each day, I'd pull one of those trees out, pull the branches out to fluff it up, and attach a tag to it that said "HOLD for Dave Bamberger's mother-in-law." Then I'd drag it to the back of the tent where the guys unloaded the trees and set it aside, like it was something really special.

When the right customers walked in, I'd start chatting with them, really buttering them up. Then I'd tell them that I could see they needed something special. I'd lead them to the back of the tent, where I had stashed that tree I tagged for my mother-in-law, and I would pull it out. I'd yank off the tag and spin the tree around once or twice to show it off. "I'm going to let you have this one," I'd say, twirling it one more time. "I'm not that crazy about my mother-in-law anyway. To hell with her. I'm going to sell it to you."

The customer would eat it up. They were going to get the very tree that the one and only J. David Bamberger, cofounder of Church's Chicken, was saving for his mother-in-law? That must be some special tree. I would load that tree onto their car, and they'd drive off happy. And as soon as they were gone, I'd go grab another tree and set it aside, too.

—⁄ı＼—

David's Christmas tree story comes with a postscript. A few weeks after we went to the tree lot, I was staying at Selah. David knocked on the door to say hi with a sheet of paper in his hand. He wanted me to read a letter he had received from Brian, one of the young men who was working at the tree lot that day we visited. We read the letter together: "I remember the first time you walked up to the tree lot, and normally I find the members just sitting in the trailer, sipping on a warm cup of coffee. Not you!" Brian wrote.

David, he explained in the letter, would rake tree needles, trim tree branches, and find creative opportunities to sell trees to customers while the others relaxed. "I found out rapidly that no one leaves the lot without a tree," Brian wrote. "You saw beauty in every tree and had a thought that if they left without a tree, they would be then spending their money somewhere else." David also realized that even if he sold a tree at a lesser price, that customer likely would return the next year. And the year after.

David taught Brian about closing a sale, but as they chatted between sales, he passed on a whole lot more—stories about the importance of grass and birds and the need to control cedar tree growth had stuck with him. Brian gleaned hours of advice about how to lead a productive life. "I took those stories and found a way to start my path down this life, learning from you that every opportunity is just a steppingstone to the next and to treat every breath as if it could be my last," he wrote.

Have You Ever Been Unsuccessful?

Most people look at J. David Bamberger and see a pretty successful guy. He grew up poor but discovered a talent for sales as a door-to-door vacuum cleaner salesman. Later, he made millions in the fast-food business. Then he bought a worn-out ranch and transformed it into a healthy, green-tinted oasis where springs

David at the guesthouse at Selah, telling Pam stories from the good old days.
Photo by Pam LeBlanc.

flow, bats populate a human-made cavern, and trees flourish.

An array of organizations, including the Texas Commission on Environmental Quality, the Texas Parks and Wildlife Department, the Texas Forest Service, the Sand County Foundation, the Texas Chapter of the Wildlife Society, and the Garden Club of America, have recognized his conservation and land stewardship work. A row of signs recognizing his achievements lines the driveway leading from the front gate to the main ranch buildings. So what has he ever done that did not work out?

～✦～

I'm embarrassed at the amount of publicity I've gotten over the years. One year—I think it was 1996—I'm at this party, and everybody is sitting around with a drink in their hand. We're talking about things people have done and somebody asks me, "Bamberger, did you ever do anything that wasn't successful?"

"Yes," I told him. "If you're trying to build a business, you're not always going to be successful." The man then asked me to tell the group one specific thing I'd done that hadn't been successful. Of course there were lots of things I did that weren't successful. But he was referring to business mistakes. I thought for a few minutes about the things that had made up my life so far. I had the ranch, of course, and my career at Church's. That all looked pretty good.

But there's one thing that I hadn't been so good at. I knew the answer to his question. I said to him, "Well, my first marriage broke up." And I mean this shocked people, because they all knew me and Margaret and thought we'd been together forever. For twenty seconds, nothing but pure silence hung in the air. Finally, after the quiet dissolved, somebody asked me how long my first marriage had lasted. I told the truth: forty-five years. A pause, and then laughter. "Shit," someone said. "That was successful."

-⁄|\-

Playing Poker with the Guys

I'm leaning over a counter inside Hes' Country Store on a mild November afternoon, watching seven men gathered around a long table slap down cards and laugh. This scene has unfolded, in more or less similar fashion, once a year for more than half a century. Technically, it is a poker game. In reality, it is much more. These guys have seen each other through marriages and births, careers and deaths. They have told jokes, sipped beer, swapped stories, and shared dreams. One night every year they gather around a table together, no matter what, to catch up. Of course, poker night also involves a lot of smack talk and tall-tale telling.

David, his brother Tom, and a few friends started playing back in the 1960s, during David's Kirby sweeper days. The first few times, they convened in East Texas, which at the time was part of David's vacuum cleaner sales territory. Later the game moved

David and his friends gather annually for a long-standing poker game at Selah. Photo by Pam LeBlanc.

to David's ranch in Bulverde. Forty-eight years ago, it came here, to Selah. The men liked it because they got out of the city. They could cut up with no one watching, and they all brought pockets loaded with small bills. They would tease and cuss and drink and joke while the sun set, the moon rose, and the stars came out.

They would keep playing, sometimes, until the sun cast its first rosy rays the next morning.

Other than David, all those original players are dead now, which means, in a way, his friends now joke, that David finally won. He is playing today with the sons of those original players, or people he met later on, just thirty or forty years ago. A fire blazes in the old potbellied stove. Antiques—that old cannonball, a box of "vermin killer," an assortment of old kitchen tools—line the walls. I am always drawn to that stuff, because it is a direct line back to David's early days, growing up in Ohio. I will pull something off the shelf, hold it in my hand, and think about what role it played in somebody's life decades earlier. It makes everything in my life seem so new and disposable.

In recent years, the poker game has coincided with a barbecue that David hosts for the hunters who lease part of Selah each deer season. It is pushing evening now, and the hunters have mostly dispersed. Outside, someone is wrapping up scraps of brisket and sausage and packing up the empty pie pans. The picnic tables are empty; the hunters have gone back to the Recycle Cabin, a modest little structure furnished with hand-me-down

Most of the bets are for one dollar or five dollars. Photo by Pam LeBlanc.

couches, tables, and chairs, where they stay when they come. Others head back to their campsites.

But here inside Hes' store, things are just gearing up. It's about 4:00 p.m., and some of these players will stick around all night, until they have depleted the snack supply and drained the beer. Pots might grow to $150, but probably not much more. "Come on baby, I need this!" David hollers from his post at the head of the table. He flips a card over and slides it into his hand, trying not to give anything away.

David's son David K. is leaning over the counter next to me, watching and reminiscing about the early days. When he was twelve or thirteen, he watched the original group play. Many of those early players were World War II veterans. Back then, pots might swell to twelve hundred dollars or so. Big money, especially back then. David K. looks over at his dad, who is telling a joke that has everyone at the table busting out in laughter.

"They were an exuberant bunch," David K. says. "I like to

David and his son David K. chat outside Hes' Country Store the day of the 2018 poker game. Photo by Pam LeBlanc.

come to these gatherings because I still get a flashback to those days. They'd seen hell and lived through it. They just had a different way of approaching things." He senses the same thing I do. That even though this is just a poker game, so much knowledge and experience are huddled around that table right now, though you would not guess it based on the steady stream of jokes and nonsense we are hearing.

"Speaking for myself, I feel an overwhelming sense that there's a legacy to pass on here," David K. says. He's right. David K. tells me about his memories of this poker game. His uncle Tom, David's brother, would come down from Oklahoma, serious as heck about the card game. Another man, a friend of David's who served as a cook in the military, would cook up a pot of chili. That man's son is here at the table now, waving a handful of cards and poking fun at David. "We'd watch 'em and listen to them yell until we fell asleep," David K. says.

Donnie Stowe, seventy-one, one of the guys gathered around the table today, is here, as he says, to represent his father, Otis, a friend of David's from before the fried-chicken days. Donnie has been playing since the game moved to Selah. "My father and I used to come together," he tells me now. "My parents were part-time gamblers. I kind of learned from them. It was exciting—a friendly game with a lot of people."

Once, Stowe walked away with eighteen hundred dollars. Last year, he pocketed sixty dollars. Another time, he lost just about all the cash he brought to play. On the drive home the next day, he jokes, he had to share a hamburger with another of the players because he could not afford to buy his own. "You never know," Stowe says. "It's the friendship, the jokes, just getting out in the country."

Some of the men tell me they set aside a little money every year as a sort of slush fund for the game. Some show up with seven hundred or eight hundred dollars in their pocket. They are tossing out one-dollar bills now, plus the occasional five dollars. The rules are pretty simple: five-dollar raises, with a maximum of three raises.

"Don't worry. David won't be in it much longer," someone

The poker game continues into the night. Photo by Pam LeBlanc

jokes. "It's past his nap time." But David keeps playing. Then he breaks into song. Everyone groans. Eyeballs roll. "If that were me, I'd fold," someone wryly advises.

"The education center needs a new window," someone else yells out, egging him on. David has been raising money to build a new research facility at the ranch for the last year, and the structure is finally rising from the ground. All the players know he has been hustling donations to cover the project.

David K. and I chuckle from our post at the counter. "It's the same bullshit every year," David K. tells me, only I am getting the sanitized version. As soon as I leave, David K. tells me, the guys will really get down to business. The chanting will begin. Anyone who wins a hand will receive a hail of four-letter words. I think about walking outside long enough for everyone to forget I am here. Then I could sit under the window, which is propped open with a long wooden pole, and listen to the ruckus. But I leave them to their fun. I have been around only a couple of years. I have not earned my spot quite yet.

Betting on LBJ

Selah is not far from Johnson City, where Lyndon Baines Johnson was born in a wood-planked farmhouse and which lies just down the road from Stonewall. Bamberger loves to play pranks, and he can pull a story out of his pocket like the next guy pulls out a handkerchief, such as this one about the thirty-sixth president of the United States, who served from 1963 to 1969. The dates are hazy, but it must have happened after Johnson's presidency, when both men were practically neighbors.

⁓

Lyndon Johnson's neighbor was the daughter of a friend of mine. She married one of Johnson's relatives, and the entire Optimist Club got invited to the wedding reception. I already had Selah, so this was around 1970. At the reception, I'm talking to the guys from the club, blowing smoke about my new ranch just down the road. I tell them I know LBJ. They don't believe me, of course, so I tell them I'm taking bets. Each of these guys puts up five dollars, and I throw in another twenty dollars. They think I'm making it up, and it's true. I don't know Johnson, except from pictures in the newspaper.

But there's a dance floor, and Johnson's on the other side of it, across the room. I tell the guys, "I'm going over to talk to him." They're all standing there, thinking they've got my twenty dollars. I walk across the dance floor toward LBJ. He's a big guy, and he sees me coming, so I stick out my arm like I'm going to shake hands with an old friend. He thinks I'm a donor or a constituent, but he doesn't really know me. I just smile real big, and when I get over there, he puts his hand on my shoulder. From way across the room, where my friends are watching this unfold, it looks like we're old friends. I ham it up. I tell him I've bought the old Carter place next to him. It's over in two minutes, but I win that bet.

—⁓⁓—

Smitten with Ann

Ann Richards, the forty-fifth—and second female—governor of Texas, looms large in state lore. She wore a white helmet of hair and dropped one-liners like delicate yet powerful bombs. Texas appreciated her first, but the whole country got its first real taste of Ann in 1988, when she delivered the keynote address at the Democratic National Convention. That speech was studded with zingers, such as "I'm delighted to be here with you this evening, because after listening to George Bush all these years, I figured you needed to know what a real Texas accent sounds like." In July 1992, she famously appeared on the cover of *Texas Monthly* magazine, perched on a motorcycle, wearing a fringe-trimmed white leather jacket and pants, next to a headline that read "White Hot Mama." Years later, Richards, who loved films, appeared in a clip shown before showtime at the Alamo Drafthouse theaters, warning people to keep quiet during the movies. In the bit, she fielded an emergency phone call, then headed to the theater, where she marched down the aisle and tossed out the offending customer. The clip wrapped with the words "Don't talk during the movies or Ann Richards will take your ass out" scrolling across the screen.

That kind of larger-than-life attitude appealed to David. He had a pretty large attitude himself.

—⁓—

I met Ann Richards when Andy Sansom, then head of the Texas Parks and Wildlife Department, brought her to the ranch after she became governor in 1991. She came out here with all of Andy's higher-ups. He needed a place for a meeting, and he thought it was appropriate to bring her out on the land as opposed to a hotel.

I thought she was wonderful. I was single at the time, and I enjoyed the hell out of her. Before she left, I presented her with a jar of honey, made here at Selah. Ten days later, I got a letter from her. It said something like, "The jar of honey's good, and so are you." Then I got a call from her appointment secretary and ended up being named chairman of the International Trade Commission for the State of Texas. I wasn't qualified, but they said, "Aw, Bamberger, there's nothing to it." Ann also asked me to serve on a private landowner board we created back then (now called the Private Lands and Habitat Program). The board provided advice on conservation and creating wildlife habitat.

The next thing that happened was I got an invitation to float the Rio Grande with Ann. I wasn't going to go, but my secretary encouraged me, so I did. A group of us floated the Rio Grande for five days and four nights. We started in Big Bend National Park and must have had three or four big rafts, with six or seven of us on each, including lots of politicians, all paddling. We slept in tents. That was more fun. It was a wonderful trip.

Afterwards I get a call one day from Ann, asking me to come in and see her. "David," she said. "Tell me about this International Trade Commission."

I said, "Ann, it's the biggest bunch of bullshit we've got in state government." I loved this woman because she was quick to catch on.

She said, "I thought so. But why do you think so?"

I told her why. I said, "What business does the State of Texas have duplicating what the federal government already does on the federal level? Going on a mission to Japan to promote Texas products—I just call that stuff political junkets." She got rid of the International Trade Commission within nine months. I thought she was one of the best things that ever happened to Texas.

Introducing Jane Goodall to Selah

Walk the paved and gravel roads that crisscross Selah and you might spot a jackrabbit, or a rattlesnake, or a cow busily munching away in a grassy field. If you are in the right spot, you could even see a small herd of scimitar-horned oryx, a species of antelope native to Africa with long, curved horns and a slightly befuddled expression on their faces.

You will not find a chimpanzee, of course. So it might seem odd that a path that winds away from the east end of Madrone Lake bears a little wooden post with the words "Jane Goodall Trail" nailed to it. But Goodall, whose name conjures images of the researcher prowling through the jungle, her eyes laser-beamed onto a family of primates, visited Selah in the late 1990s, much to Bamberger's delight. He still talks about it now, and his respect for her is obvious. That is why he put her name on one of the ranch's most visible trails. Here is David's spin on how her visit to the ranch unfolded.

David Bamberger, Jane Goodall, and Colleen S. Gardner, now executive director of Selah, pose during Goodall's visit to the ranch. Courtesy David Bamberger.

⁓⁕⁓

Jane Goodall went to San Antonio back in 1997 or 1998 to visit a friend of hers who lived there and to speak to the local chapter of the worldwide organization called the Explorers Club. The club's members have all done amazing things, like summited Mount Everest, or slogged to the North Pole, or shed light into the deepest depths of the ocean. Jane spent more than half a century studying wild chimps in Tanzania, so, of course, she fit right in. A friend of mine in San Antonio wanted to know if they could bring her to Selah and show her around. "Can you host Jane Goodall?" he says, and I say, "Is a pig's ass pork?"

So she came. We didn't have the guesthouse then, so Margaret and I arranged for her to stay at the ranch house with us. But she refused to stay in the main house because the bedroom was air-conditioned. Instead, she stayed in what we called the "cubbyhole." When the ranch house was built in the 1930s, they put in a little room on the side of the garage where the maid stayed. I put two bunkbeds in there, but it was pretty hot.

But Jane was so easy, and Margaret, being the kind of woman she was, you'd have thought they knew one another for years. They just bonded immediately. Jane dressed casually, and there was no pretentiousness. The next day she spoke at the ranch. I invited a large group of local guests to come listen, and people poured in. How often does a world-renowned person like Jane Goodall make an appearance in Blanco County?

She talked for more than an hour about her experiences in Tanzania with the chimps. Then we loaded as many of the visitors as wanted to go onto our Bluebonnet trailer and headed out for a tour of the ranch. The dinosaur tracks were an important stop. The oryx were a big one for Jane, too. She talked about the importance of conservation and about how every person had to do their part. In her own special way, she suggested that we all stop and think before we run out and spend money on things. Humans are wasting so much energy and natural resources all over the world. We build something, and it winds up in the landfill. Before you get something, Jane said, ask yourself the question: "Do I really need it?"

Standing Up Lady Bird

I wake up in the dead of night sometimes, awakened from a recurring nightmare that I have somehow missed a final exam at college, forgotten a speaking engagement, or missed an important interview that I had scheduled weeks earlier. So I employ an intricate system of cellphone alerts, Post-it notes, and color-coded tags on my digital calendar. I am deathly afraid of forgetting appointments, including appointments with David. If we set a

David relaxes outside Hes' Country Store, November 2017. He had injured his shoulder while picking fall leaves to tuck into his annual Christmas card. Photo by Pam LeBlanc

time to meet, he likes to keep me on my toes. "What time do you want me there?" I ask him.

"6:24 p.m.," he tells me, always throwing in an oddball number.

I do my best to show up at exactly the right minute, which is pretty funny, considering that if David tells someone at the ranch he will be someplace at, say, 5:00 p.m., and if he has anyone with him who will listen to his stories, he is likely to show up at least thirty minutes late. You just learn to factor that into the equation. But there are some times when timing is everything.

⁓⁓

A number of years ago I received a phone call from Lady Bird Johnson's personal secretary, who asked if I had time to speak to Mrs. Johnson. I did, of course. "Dr. Bamberger, I'm putting together a dinner party here at the Texas White House," Mrs. Johnson said. "I didn't want to set the date until I knew you were available."

"What date are you planning for?" I asked, as if that mattered to me at all. She suggested three or four possibilities. "You can stop right there," I said. "Those are entirely open on my calendar."

I jotted down the engagement. The following day, my phone rang. It was Mrs. Johnson again. "Dr. Bamberger"—and she always called me "doctor"—"I'm sorry to bother you again," Mrs. Johnson said. "It's about our dinner party. I like to bring interesting people together for my parties, particularly ones who have accomplished things for the environment and conservation. I thought you might know of someone who fits that description that I might include in our party." I told her I knew a few people and asked her to give me a day to check with them and get back in touch. As you might expect, the first person I called immediately agreed to come. I turned the name over to Mrs. Johnson's secretary.

The date for the party was two weeks out, and things were busy at the ranch. A group of students came down from the University of Minnesota to study the migration of monarch butterflies. They brought envelopes filled with live butterflies. They'd open those envelopes, and the monarchs would unfold their wings and fly out. I loved learning about them.

The day of the party arrived, and I glanced outside. The sun was shining. I looked at Margaret and said, "Let's pack up a nice picnic along with one or two bottles of wine, go off in the old Jeep, and spend the day out on the ranch." She liked the idea, and we did just that. It was a wonderful day. It couldn't have been more perfect.

At about 6:00 p.m., as we were returning from our picnic, we stopped by the education center to say hello to the students. The stop quickly turned into a lot of interesting conversation, which progressed into dinner. Margaret and I stuck around to do the dishes, too. When we finally rolled back to the ranch house at about 8:30 p.m., the red light was blinking on the answering machine. I pushed the button. "Mr. Bamberger, this is Shirley James, Mrs. Johnson's secretary. Since you're not answering, I'm assuming you're on your way to Mrs. Johnson's dinner party."

My heart flipped. We'd totally forgotten. "Margaret, my God," I croaked. "What are we going to do?"

"David," she said. "That's your problem, not mine."

I spent a sleepless night. What do you do when you stand up a First Lady? I had promised to head to the center the next morning to see the students again. Dr. Bill Calvert, a monarch expert from the University of Texas, met me there. I told him what had happened. He gave me a few quick words of advice. "David, that's a hell of a mistake," he said. "You get in your truck, drive as fast as you can to San Antonio, check into the Methodist Hospital, and call her from there."

That wasn't a bad idea, but I couldn't do it. By midmorning, I'd gotten no help from Margaret, who wisely suggested I face the situation head-on. I picked up the phone, lay down on the tile floor in my workroom, and dialed Mrs. Johnson's number. Shirley James, the secretary, answered the phone. "Ms. James," I said sheepishly. "This is David Bamberger. I desperately need to speak to Mrs. Johnson."

"Yes, Mr. Bamberger, I think you do," she said.

Lady Bird came to the phone. "Mrs. Johnson, I'm on the floor, begging," I began. "Can you possibly forgive an old man?"

She quickly put me at ease. "Oh, Dr. Bamberger, of course I can. We had a lovely dinner party and you were missed, but I've forgotten things too. It's a part of getting old." Mrs. Johnson invited us to dinner on three more occasions. Each time, her secretary called to remind us of our date.

―⁄⁞⸜―

A Surprise Donor

David's downhome charm comes in handy, especially when he's working like a politician, trying to raise money for the cause he believes in most—land conservation. He wants Selah to exist in perpetuity, remain undeveloped, and serve as a living laboratory for students and others to study how to heal and protect the land. He has learned through the years that sometimes the least likely people are the ones who make the biggest difference and that someone who shows up to take a public tour at the ranch might just turn out to make an impact for years to come.

⸝⹁⸌

I met Don when he came on a public tour of the ranch. He looked frail, although he wasn't. A beard hung down below his chin. It was the early 1990s, before I had the Bluebonnet, and guests just rode on bales of hay on the back of a trailer. He was about sixty at the time, and every time I came to a gate, he jumped off the trailer to help me out. He really enjoyed the day. About a month later I received a check from him for $250, along with a note written on the back of an envelope. He took a used envelope he'd gotten from us in the mail and turned it over, and that was his stationery. He wrote to tell me that he and his brother were buying a piece of property in Caldwell County. He said, "Would you be so kind as to come out there and tell us how to manage it?"

I wrote back and told him, "Just tell me when."

He didn't write back, but a year later he called and said, "I'm living out here in Bastrop County now. Would you come here? I have a bat house, and I don't have any bats living in it."

Again, I said, "Just tell me when."

He gave me directions, and I called him when I got to Bastrop, offering to bring barbecue out for lunch. He said that would be wonderful, and I drove out Highway 21. From the gate back to where he lived was about a mile and a half, maybe more. The road wasn't paved. It wasn't even dirt; it was just a road on grass. I was shocked when I got there. He was living in a shack that leaned a good fifteen degrees, with one lightbulb hanging down from the ceiling and no running water. I thought to myself, "How the hell do he and his brother buy land in Caldwell County?"

The first thing he did was ask me if I'd like to go inside and eat. I'd seen that shack, so I said, "Shoot, no, let's eat outside." Then he said, "Well, we better go get us a table." We walked up a hill, a steep grade, to this old barn. It was filled with his inherited possessions. We went through all this junk and found a card table. He brought it out, and we carried it down to the shack. He looked at the table, which was covered with dirt and dust. "We need some place mats," he said. He went into his house and came out with a couple of Budweiser beer cartons and flattened them out.

But here's the real story. This guy was a graduate of the University of Texas, a geologist. Ten years earlier, he was working in Colorado, prospecting. He received a note from his father, who said, "Son, I'm getting too old for this. If you will come back home to take care of me, the farm, and the cattle, I'll see to it that it's all yours when I'm gone."

He wrote back. "Dear Father," he said. "I can do that for you, but you must get my brother and sister involved and tell them what you're doing."

That was the smartest thing he ever did in his life. His dad's place sounded like a big operation, but really it was just one hundred acres with nine cows along Interstate 35 between Austin and San Marcos. Don came home and took care of the cattle until his dad died. Then he inherited the property. Soon people started knocking on his door. And I'm telling you what he told me. They started knocking on his door with regularity, and they said things like, "My wife and I have a double wide and we're looking for a place to put it." Don got nervous about it. He didn't have any for sale signs up or anything. Fortunately, he told his lawyer about all these people who wanted to buy the property and how it bothered him.

The lawyer said, "Just send them to me." A year later, the lawyer called Don and asked him to come in so they could talk. Don sat down in his lawyer's office, which was all done up in mahogany panels. The lawyer proceeded to tell him, "I think I have something here you can't refuse." Don ended up selling that 105-acre plot to Cabela's sporting goods company for something like ten million dollars. That's where Cabela's store in Buda stands now. But the rest of the story gets even more unbelievable.

Don didn't care about all that money. He donated most of it to the Texas Parks and Wildlife Department. He set up a trust with the rest and lived off its earnings. Then he began donating to Bamberger Ranch Preserve. Every year or two we'd get a check for one, two, three, or four thousand dollars.

Then one day, I got a call from the president of my bank in Johnson City, who tells me, "Mr. Bamberger, you sure have some good friends." I know I do, but I asked him why he thought that. The bank president told me that $784,000 had just been electronically transferred into my account.

I said, "'Are you pulling my leg?'"

He confirmed it and told me the donor's name. It was Don Rylander in Bastrop. I get him on the phone. "We got this wonderful gift from you," I told him. Then he apologized. "I'm sorry. It was supposed to be one million dollars, but the bank, Wells Fargo, lost the difference and I was afraid if it kept on going, they might lose it all." He had dissolved the trust and used the money to make charitable contributions to several organizations, including Bamberger Ranch Preserve.

⁓⁄⎜⋋

When I tracked Rylander down, he told me that he had inherited that family farm in Caldwell County and explained why he did what he did. "It turned out after thirty years I was right in the way of the expansion of a city. I really did not want to sell. I enjoyed working on the farm and raising cattle, but when roads and buildings and subdivisions developed on all sides of me, I decided to sell the land and give the money to other people who could save land—and to the Texas State Parks system."

Selah was one of those places. He realized that his land on Interstate 35 would be developed and by donating to Bamberger and the parks system, he could make a sort of trade. "I'll have to get rid of my land," he told me, "but I can use my money to save other land." Besides, he respected the passion with which Bamberger tried to educate the next generation. "Bamberger takes good care of his land and he also does something I never did but should have—he tries to teach little kids about conservation," Rylander, now in his eighties, said. "It's an important thing. If you don't teach the young to take care of the land, we're going to be in a world of hurt."

Cory

Cory, a friendly red dog with yellow eyes, used to stick to David's heels wherever he went and met his gaze as often as possible. When I first started coming out to Selah, Cory would race out of the front door, David right behind him, then dash around the corner of the ranch house, checking every few seconds to make sure his sidekick was watching. When he got around back, Cory would run right up the trunk of one of the gnarled old oak trees that grew there, then glance back down, a grin on his sweet face.

He loved to climb trees, and like David, he loved an audience, too. If a group of students was out at the ranch, David would introduce them to Cory, who would promptly climb a tree. Cory kept that up as long as he could, but as he started to get older, David tried to convince him he was too old for tree climbing. After a while, he could not hop up into the back of the pickup truck so easily either. David would give him a boost, or if my husband, Chris, was around, he would hoist the friendly pup up to where he needed to go.

David and Joanna had plenty of stories to share about Cory, who would nap at David's feet while we ate lunch or sleep in the living room when the couple hosted gatherings at the ranch house. He scrapped with porcupines, joined us in the dig pit on days we looked for projectile points, and followed us as we hiked across the property. He was, as David called him, "The best dog in all of the United States of America, and Texas too."

⁓⋅⁄⋅⁓

I must have gotten him about 2002. A good friend of mine, the writer Suzy Banks, loved dogs. She knew we were looking for one, so now and then she'd call us up and say she had a stray to show us. She'd load the animal into her car and drive it over. We'd tell her no; we couldn't have a longhaired dog like that on a ranch. A week or two later, she'd call with another one for us to see. She'd drive out here again, and we'd reject that dog for some other reason, too. After a while, we had to

Cory, who was known for his ability to climb trees, naps, March 2016. Photo by Pam LeBlanc.

describe for her exactly what kind of dog we were look-ing for—one that was a little bigger than the last one, maybe, one with shorter hair and a pleasant disposition.

One day she called us and said that while she was at the veterinarian's office, a woman had come in with

David lifts Cory into the back of his Toyota pickup truck, 2017. Photo by Pam LeBlanc.

a medium-sized red dog that had showed up at her doorstep. The woman kept the dog for a few days but couldn't give it a permanent home. She wanted the vet to check and see if it was chipped, so she could return it to its owner. Suzy overheard this whole exchange. She took one look at that dog and knew. She introduced herself to the woman and announced that if nobody could find the dog's owner, she knew the perfect couple and the perfect place for that dog—on our ranch in Blanco County.

It turns out the dog wasn't chipped and the people at the veterinarian's office couldn't find an owner. The woman who had found the dog called me up and told me she was headed to Santa Fe, New Mexico. She said she'd drop the dog by, if we wanted, along with food enough to last for two weeks. She told us she'd call us again when she was heading back from New Mexico to see what we thought. "If you don't want him, I'll take him back," she said.

A day or two later, she brought us Cory. He was exactly what we wanted. We took to him immediately. And then he tried to kill a goat. Margaret was with him when that happened, and she got him off the goat and called me. I came down. The next day I put a collar and a long rope on the dog and took him down to look at the goats again. Every time he started to lunge, I jerked the rope. After three or four days of that, he didn't kill goats anymore.

Well, we just fell in love with him. And we started calling him Cory, for Canine of Red hair and Yellow eyes. In about two weeks, the woman came back from Santa Fe. When she got close to the ranch, she called and left us a phone message. I immediately called her back.

David and Cory sit at the edge of Madrone Lake, 2017. Photo by Pam LeBlanc.

Cory rides in the back of David's pickup truck, May 2016. Photo by Pam LeBlanc.

"Don't you dare come by here," I said. "Don't you dare. This is our dog, and we love him."

Cory fit right in at Selah. I taught him to jump up into the back of a pickup truck, and he drives all around the ranch with me. One day we were walking on a trail around Madrone Lake. A squirrel jumped out in front of me, and he took off after it. He chased that squirrel, and the squirrel darted right up a tree. The next thing I know, the dog climbed into the tree too. That became his trademark move.

Handing Over the Reins

"I can't believe the life I've had," David told me one evening at the ranch house in late September 2016. It was the day after a party held at the site of the new Margaret Bamberger Research and Education Center, and he was standing at the island in the kitchen of the ranch house, pulling out plates and silverware for dinner.

He shook his head, like he could not believe how far he had come. Because, really, how could it have turned out this way? How could someone born into poverty spend seventeen years as a door-to-door vacuum salesman, build a trio of tiny fried-chicken stores into a worldwide chain, then buy this ranch, where people came to learn how to heal land that has been neglected or over-worked?

But it happened, and David, who was eighty-nine at the time, knew he did not have many years left on this planet. He was trying to prepare Selah for what would happen next, and he wanted to make sure that people continued to come here to learn about land conservation, even after he was gone. The night before, he told me, was a big test.

For days, the staff had bustled around, getting ready for the party. David could not stop worrying about it. It did not matter that he had hosted dozens of events like this before—this would mark the first time that he let someone else lead the show. Honestly, he struggled a little giving up that control, even though he knew it was time. "I'd always felt like the general, and I was concerned the staff wouldn't execute it the way I would if I was doing it myself," he told me. "But for the last two or three years, I've been nervous about my health, especially after the spells that sent me to Houston for six months," he told me. "I've been anxious. I've been wondering—are these people ready to totally take over?"

Hours before the party, to thank people who had donated to the construction of the new center, David walked out onto the patio slab as the staff made final preparations. They had arranged picnic tables, sunk posts into the ground, and wired electricity to them. They had put up a temporary stage made of lumber salvaged from recent floods on the Blanco River. Margaret's photo was displayed, and a small wall set up to show donors what the walls of the new education center would look like. Steven had caught enough catfish to feed the seventy-five or so guests.

David went outside and walked around, checking everything out. Then he went back inside and found Joanna. "These young people have everything in place," he told her. "I didn't have anything to critique."

She looked back at David and smiled. "David, you can die now," she said.

Later that evening, after the guests had arrived, the catfish was frying, and the music had started, David pulled Colleen Gardner, Selah's executive director, aside and told her he had a slight change in plans. He wanted to take the microphone after all. He promised to take just one minute. Colleen no doubt raised an eyebrow at that, because David was not known for his brevity. Still, she handed over the microphone, and David told the group gathered before him what he now refers to as the "You Can Die Now Story."

Then he gave the microphone back to Colleen, who related a story about how the huge cathedrals of Europe were constructed.

The builders, she told the crowd, never saw the finished cathedral, because it took so long to construct. Then she said, "You're on the pad of David Bamberger's cathedral."

The original cathedral was a vision; then someone laid down the stone. Later someone built a roof, and someone else added the art. Colleen walked everyone through that story and then told them that David would not start building the cathedral until he had at least half a million dollars. At the time, they had raised $470,500. The party was not meant to be a fundraiser, but donors contributed $68,000 more that night. They had enough to start building.

That night ushered in the next chapter of David's legacy. David wanted the Margaret Bamberger Research and Education Center to spearhead a complete biological survey of every living thing at Selah. The study would take a decade and shift the emphasis of Selah's educational work slightly, from elementary-age children to high school and college students. Through their research, he hoped to scientifically quantify changes taking place in the environment.

At one point, David's net worth approached fifty million dollars, and he owned more than seven thousand acres of land. But that is not what is most important to him. "If I wanted to be known for something, I really don't want to be known for Church's. Yes, that made a lot of things possible, but it ended in 1988. My God, that was thirty years ago."

When he dies, the biggest part of what he has left will go to the Bamberger Ranch Preserve to build an endowment. A smaller family foundation will inherit his ranch house, everything in it, and an easement around it. David's family will decide what to do with the house, but one day it could become a sort of museum, like Hes' Country Store. "This sounds so egotistical, but that country store with my mom's name on it? It's an unbelievable home run in teaching children to conserve their heritage. It motivates so many people," he said.

He can picture families, years from now, dropping by the main ranch house on a hill, seeing his reading glasses resting on a table there or a few Native American artifacts he found on the property. And just maybe, he says, it will motivate them to carry on the work he started here in the Texas Hill Country. As development encroaches and ranches are subdivided, he envisions Selah as an oasis, the Central Park of Blanco County.

"You can put a new roof on the Alamodome; you can buy new buses or cars," he said. "With land you can't do that. When you consume land, it's gone. Gone forever."

INDEX